WHEN I AM AFRAID

KAY ARTHUR
JANNA ARNDT

HARVEST HOUSE PUBLISHERS
EUGENE, OREGON

Cover design by Left Coast Design
Interior design by Janelle Coury
Illustrations by Steve Bjorkman

For bulk, special sales, or ministry purchases, please call 1-800-547-8979.
Email: CustomerService@hhpbooks.com

This logo is a federally registered trademark of the Hawkins Children's LLC. Harvest House Publishers, Inc., is the exclusive licensee of this trademark.

DISCOVER 4 YOURSELF is a federally registered trademark of the Hawkins Children's LLC. Harvest House Publishers, Inc., is the exclusive licensee of this trademark.

When I Am Afraid

Copyright © 2024 by Precept Ministries International and Janna Arndt
Published by Harvest House Publishers
Eugene, Oregon 97408
www.harvesthousepublishers.com

ISBN 978-0-7369-8872-8 (pbk.)

Printed in the United States of America

24 25 26 27 28 29 30 31 32 / VP / 10 9 8 7 6 5 4 3 2 1

For Mia and Costel Oglice,
for your faithfulness, so children all over the world
will know and love God's Word.

I thank my God in all my remembrance of you,
always offering prayer with joy in my every prayer for you all...
For I am confident of this very thing,
that He who began a good work in you will perfect it
until the day of Christ Jesus.
PHILIPPIANS 1:3-4, 6

For the children in the Ukraine and for children all over the world,
so they will know that when they are afraid, they can put their
trust in God.

In peace I will both lie down and sleep,
for You alone, O LORD, make me to dwell in safety.
PSALM 4:8

And for my precious grandchildren, Oliver, Hal, and Josie.
I am so very thankful God blessed me with you!

Be strong and courageous! Do not tremble or be dismayed,
for the LORD your God is with you wherever you go.
JOSHUA 1:9

I love you with all my heart! —Granna

CONTENTS

CONQUERING FEAR—

A BIBLE STUDY *YOU* CAN DO!

Hi! Are you ready to go on a new Bible adventure at Camp Braveheart to find out WHAT you should do when you feel afraid? There are many difficult things in our world that can cause you to feel afraid and alone. Sometimes when you leave home to have fun at camp you may feel a little nervous and afraid. What if you don't know anyone? At other times, you may have to leave home because something bad has happened, like a tornado, a fire, a hurricane, or a war.

Whether you are leaving home for a fun adventure like camp or because something hard and difficult has happened, leaving home may feel scary and very hard.

Did you know the Bible, God's book, talks a lot about being afraid? As you begin your new Bible adventure you will discover WHAT God says about being afraid, and HOW different people in the Bible handled their fears.

Do you know WHO becomes afraid in a sudden storm? Or HOW David had the courage to stand up to a giant? WHO goes to God and asks for help when there is a battle and he doesn't know what to do? WHO is in control of all your circumstances?

WHO can help you when you are scared and bad things happen to you?

HOW can you trust God when you feel anxious and afraid?

You'll find out the answers to all these questions by studying God's Word, the Bible—the source of all truth—and by asking God's Spirit to lead and guide you. You also have this book, which is an inductive Bible study. That word *inductive* means you go straight to the Bible *yourself* to investigate what the Bible shows you about being afraid. In inductive Bible study you *Discover 4 Yourself* what the Bible says and means. God gives us a promise in the Bible that nothing is too difficult for Him. This is what God says, "Behold, I am the LORD, the God of all flesh; is anything too difficult for Me?" Jeremiah 32:27.

Isn't that AWESOME! Nothing is too hard for God. In life there are many hard and difficult things that make us feel lonely and afraid, but nothing is too hard for God.

Grab your Bible, God's Map, to discover the truth about an AWESOME God and an AMAZING Savior, and what it means to trust them no matter what your circumstances are. God and Jesus love you!

Follow God's Map, His plan is always for your good. WHEN you trust God and Jesus you will have a brave heart!

THINGS YOU'LL NEED

NEW AMERICAN STANDARD BIBLE
(1995 EDITION—PREFERABLY THE
NEW INDUCTIVE STUDY BIBLE)

PEN OR PENCIL

COLORED PENCILS

INDEX CARDS

A DICTIONARY

THIS WORKBOOK

WEEK 1

WHY ARE YOU AFRAID?

Welcome to Camp Braveheart! We are so happy you want to join us on our new Bible adventure to learn about being afraid. Can you name something that makes you feel afraid? HOW does being afraid make you feel? Does it make your heart beat fast? Does feeling afraid make you feel worried or anxious?

Fear is a normal emotion. We are all afraid of something. We might fear snakes, getting sick, being alone, or being in a very bad

storm. Since fear is a normal feeling we all have, it's very important to know WHAT to do when you are afraid. That's why we are excited to have you here at Camp Braveheart to discover WHAT the Bible says about being afraid and what you are to do when you are afraid.

WHY is the Bible the best place to learn about being afraid? It's because the Bible is God's book. In the Bible, 2 Timothy 3:16 tells us, "All Scripture is inspired by God." That word *inspired* means "God-breathed." All Scripture is breathed by God. Isn't that cool? God's book, the Bible, is also called God's Word. You can trust what the Bible says about being afraid because the Bible doesn't just *contain* God's words, the Bible *is* God's Word. The Bible is the truth. To conquer fear you have to know truth.

So, HOW did God's Word get written down? Second Peter 1:20-21 tells us that ordinary men were chosen by God and moved by God's Spirit telling them what to write down so we would have the very words of God. Not words about God, but God's very words.

Isn't that awesome? You are going to learn what God says about Himself and what He says about being afraid.

WHO CAN YOU TRUST?

All right! Are you settled in? Now that you have unpacked your bag, let's go meet our team, Team Truth, and get started on our Bible adventure. WHAT is the first thing you should do before you get started? Do you know? PRAY! Bible study should always start with prayer! Prayer is talking and listening to God. You need to talk to God and ask Him to help you understand what the Bible says and to teach you how to obey it as you begin your new Bible adventure. So, pray!

Now that you have prayed, what's next? Look at your map! You got it! You don't want to get lost! You need to open God's Map, the Bible. The first location we need to look at is in the book of John, which is in the New Testament part of the Bible. Let's read John 1:1-2, 14 and answer the 5 Ws and an H questions.

WHAT are the 5 Ws and an H? They are the WHO, WHAT, WHERE, WHEN, WHY, and HOW questions to help us discover what the Bible is saying.

1. Asking WHO helps you find out:
   WHO wrote this?
   WHO was it written to?
   WHO are we reading about?
   WHO said this or did that?

2. WHAT helps you understand:
   WHAT is the author talking about?
   WHAT are the main things that
   happen?

3. WHERE helps you learn:
   WHERE did something happen?
   WHERE did they go?
   WHERE was this said?
   When we discover a "WHERE" we
   double underline the "WHERE" in green.

4. WHEN tells us about time. We mark it with a green
   circle ◯ or a green clock like this: 🕒. WHEN tells us:
   WHEN did this event happen? (Or WHEN will it
   happen?)
   WHEN did the main characters do something?
   It helps us to follow the order of events.

5. WHY asks questions like:
   WHY did he say that?
   WHY did this happen?
   WHY did they go there?

6. HOW lets you figure out things like:
   HOW something is to be done or
   HOW people knew something had happened.

Now that you know what the 5 Ws and an H are, turn to your Observation Worksheets on page 223. Observation Worksheets are pages that have the Bible text printed out for you to use as you do your study.

Let's mark God's Map. Read John 1:1-2 and John 1:14 on page 223 and color the word *Word* yellow. Don't forget to mark your pronouns!

Now answer the 5 Ws and an H questions below.

John 1:1 WHO was in the beginning?

_____ _____

List WHAT you see about the Word in John 1:1.

1. The Word was in the _____.

2. The Word _____ _____ God.

3. The Word was _____.

Did you notice the Word was not only with God, but also the Word was God? The Word and God were both together in the beginning.

Look at John 1:14. WHO became flesh and dwelt among us?

_____ _____

WHAT else do you see about the Word in verse 14?

We saw His _____ as of the o __ __ __

_____ from the _____, full

of _____ and _____ .

AWESOME! So, WHO is the Word? WHO became flesh and dwelt among us? WHO is God's only begotten Son, WHO is also God?

Do you know? If you do, say it out loud. If you aren't sure, use the compass below to discover WHO the Word is.

Look at the first blank on page 17. It has a number under it. Find the number on the compass below and then place the letter in that box on the first blank.

Next, using that first letter as a starting point, follow the compass directions under the other blanks to find the rest of the letters for that word. To help you get started, we did the first one for you.

COMPASS CODE

Compass key: N = north or up, S = south or down, E = east or right, W = west or left. NW, SW, SE, and NE mean you move diagonally.

J — — — —
1 SE NE W N

    You did it! You just discovered WHO the Word is. The Word is Jesus! Are you wondering WHY John called Jesus the *Word*? It's because *Word* can mean *message*. The Bible is sometimes called God's Word because it is God's written message about Himself and His Son, Jesus. John called Jesus the Word because Jesus served as God's message about Himself to the world. God sent Jesus to show us the truth about WHO God and Jesus are. Isn't that amazing?

    Jesus was in the beginning with God.

    Jesus was God.

    Jesus is God's only begotten Son, full of grace and truth.

    Jesus left heaven to become a man to live among us.

    Jesus is God's message to the world about Himself and God.

WHAT else can you learn about Jesus? Turn to page 223 and read John 1:28-29.

John 1:28 WHO was baptizing? _____

John 1:29 WHAT did John say when he saw Jesus coming to him?

Behold, the _____ of _____.

John 1:29 WHAT does the Lamb of God do?

_____

God sent Jesus into the world to die on a cross to take away the sins of the whole world. Jesus is the Lamb of God who came to save us. God loves us so much that He gave us Jesus His only son to save us!

Isn't that wonderful! Now grab your compass to discover this week's memory verse. Each week in our Bible adventure we will have a new verse so we can learn to hide God's Word in our heart.

To discover this week's verse look at the message on page 19. Turn back to page 16 and find the compass. You will solve this verse using the same compass and the same way you discovered WHO the Word is on page 17. The first blank of each word has a number under it. Find the number on the compass and then place the letter in that box on the blank.

Next, using that first letter as a starting point, follow the compass directions under the other blanks to find the rest of the letters for that word. To help you get started, we did the first one for you.

COMPASS CODE

Compass key: N = north or up, S = south or down, E = east or right, W = west or left. NW, SW, SE, and NE mean you move diagonally.

"D __   __ __ __   __ __   __ __ __ __ __
  2 NE   3 SE E   4 SE   5 N SE E SW W

__ __ __   __ __ __ __ __ __,   __ __ __ __
 6 SW E   7 SE S W S W   8 N W S

__ __ __ __ __ __ __."   **Mark 5:36**
 9 NW SW S NE S E

Great work! In Mark 5:35 the synagogue official is told not to bother Jesus because his daughter has died. But in Mark 5:36 Jesus overhears and tells the synagogue official, "Do not be afraid any longer, only believe."

To believe Jesus means to put your trust in Him, to commit to Him, to accept what He says about someone or something, and to have faith.

HOW can the synagogue official trust Jesus? WHAT are some things you learned about Jesus today? WHO did you discover Jesus is in John 1:1-2, 14?

Jesus is G __ d.

Jesus is God's only

b __ __ __ __ __ __ __   S __ n.

God sent Jesus, the L __ __ b of God to save us from our

s __ __ s.

God and Jesus love you! You can trust Jesus because you know WHO Jesus is!

WHAT did Jesus say to the synagogue official? Write out Jesus's words on a piece of paper. Now practice saying these words out loud, three times in a row, three times every day.

WHEN you are afraid, WHAT did Jesus say to do?

B __ __ __ __ __ e! Put your trust in Jesus!

DAY TWO

A STORMY SEA

Rise and shine! Let's grab some breakfast before we head out on our hike. Yesterday we discovered WHO Jesus is, today we need to find out WHAT is happening with Jesus and His twelve disciples. WHO are the twelve disciples? The twelve disciples are the men Jesus called to follow Him. They are Jesus's closest friends.

Today we are going to open God's Map to the book of Mark, which is also in the New Testament. At this time, Jesus's disciples have been following Jesus for two years. The disciples have seen Jesus do some very amazing things like turning water into wine, healing the blind and the sick, raising the dead, and feeding the multitude with only five barley loaves and two fish! Isn't Jesus AWESOME?

Pray and ask God to help you understand and do what His Word says.

Great! Let's find out WHAT is happening in Mark 4.

One way we can uncover clues as we read the Bible is to look at the key words in the passage of Scripture we are studying and mark them in a special way.

What are *key words*? Key words are words that pop up more than once. They are called key words because they help unlock the meaning of the chapter or book you are studying and give you clues about what is most important in a passage of Scripture.

- Key words are usually used over and over again. (That's because God doesn't want you to miss the point.)

- Key Words are important.

- Key words are used by the writer for a reason.

Once you discover a key word, you need to mark it in a special way using a special color or symbol so you can immediately spot it in the Scripture. You also need to mark any pronouns for those words too! WHAT are pronouns? Check out the word box below.

PRONOUNS

Pronouns are words that take the place of nouns. A noun is a person, place, or thing. A pronoun stands in for a noun! Look at the two sentences below. Watch how the pronoun *he* is substituted for Max's name in the second sentence.

Max can't wait to discover what Jesus is doing by the sea. *He* wants to find out what happens in the boat.

The word *he* is a pronoun because it takes the place of Max's name in the second sentence. *He* is another word we use to refer to Max.

Watch for these other pronouns when you are marking people:

I	you	he	she
me	you	him	her
mine	yours	his	hers
we	it		
our	its		
they	them		

Now that you know what key words and pronouns are, turn to your Observation Worksheets on page 223. Read Mark 4:1-2 and mark every reference to *Jesus* and any pronouns for *Jesus* in a special way, just like we have listed below.

Jesus (He, Him) (draw a purple cross and color it yellow)

Mark anything that tells you WHERE by double underlining the WHERE in green.

All right! Now that you have marked Jesus in the first two verses, let's find out WHAT Jesus is doing and WHERE He is by asking the 5 Ws and an H questions.

Mark 4:1 WHAT did Jesus begin to do?

_____

WHO is Jesus teaching? A very _____ _____

Mark 4:1 WHERE is Jesus? In a _____

Now turn back to your observation worksheet on page 223. Read Mark 4:35-41 and mark the key words listed below.

Jesus (He, Teacher) (draw a purple cross and color it yellow)

disciples (they/them) (color it blue)

afraid (draw a black jagged circle around it)

Don't forget to mark your pronouns! And mark anything that tells you WHERE by double underlining the <u>WHERE</u> in green. Mark anything that tells you WHEN by drawing a green circle ○ or a green clock like this: 🕐

Tomorrow we will ask the 5 Ws and an H questions to find out WHAT happens next.

Why don't you draw a picture in the box below to show how you feel when you are afraid. WHAT does your face look like?

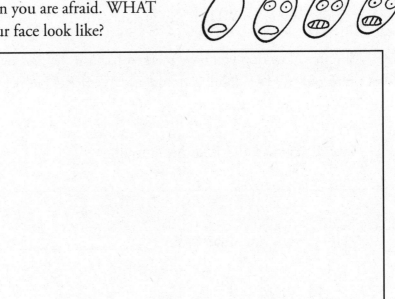

WHAT did you learn from your memory verse? WHAT should you do when you are afraid? Say it out loud! WHO are you to believe and put your trust in? Say it out loud!

Way to go!

WHAT HAPPENS IN THE STORM?

Whew! It's hot today! Let's go sit by the lake and find out WHAT is happening with Jesus and His disciples in the boat. All right Team Truth, do you remember what you need to do first?

P __ __ y! That's right! Don't forget to talk to God and ask Him to guide you as you study His book, the Bible.

Yesterday you marked your key words for Mark 4:35-41. Today, let's turn back to page 223 and read Mark 4:35-41 to find out what is happening. Ask the 5 Ws and an H questions.

Mark 4:35 WHEN is this happening?

_____

Mark 4:35 WHAT did Jesus say to the disciples?

_____

Mark 4:36 HOW are they going to the other side?

In a _____

Mark 4:36 WHO did they leave as they got into the boat?

The _____

Mark 4:37 WHAT happens while they are on the sea?

_____

Mark 4:37 WHAT was happening to the boat?

_____

Mark 4:38 WHERE is Jesus? In the _____

Mark 4:38 WHAT is Jesus doing during the storm?

_____

Mark 4:38 WHAT did the disciples do?

_____

Mark 4:38 WHAT did the disciples say to Jesus?

"Teacher, do You not _____ that we are

_____?"

Mark 4:39 WHAT did Jesus do?

_____

Mark 4:39 WHAT did Jesus say?

"Hush, _____ _____."

Mark 4:39 WHAT happened?

_____

Mark 4:40 WHAT did Jesus say to them?

"Why are _____ _____? Do you still

have _____ _____?"

Mark 4:41 WHAT did the disciples become?

_____

WHAT did they say?

"Who then is this, that even the _____ and the

_____ _____ Him?"

WHAT emotion did the disciples have?

_____

Was this a normal emotion for them to have in this situation?

_____

WHY do you think Jesus asked them, "Why are you afraid? Do you still have no faith?" The disciples have been following Jesus for two years. They have seen Him do all kinds of signs (miracles) like healing, raising the dead, and providing food. They have seen Jesus's awesome power!

Should they be afraid since Jesus is with them in the storm?

_____

Did you notice the disciples asked Jesus if He cared they were perishing (dying)? Fear causes doubt. Since the disciples know WHO Jesus is, they should know Jesus cares about them.

WHAT should the disciples have done?

_____

Draw a picture of Jesus and the disciples in the boat. Show Jesus calming the winds and the waves in the storm.

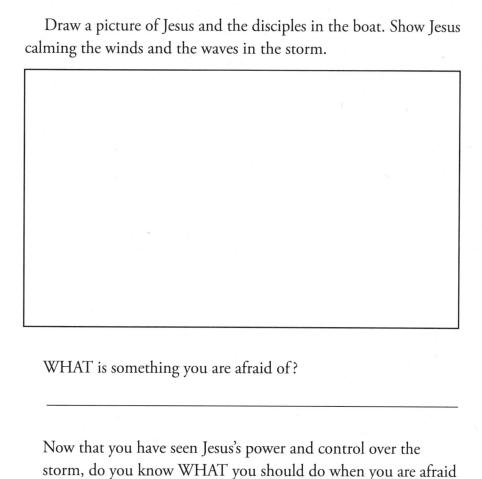

WHAT is something you are afraid of?

_____

Now that you have seen Jesus's power and control over the storm, do you know WHAT you should do when you are afraid the next time? Write out WHAT you should do when you are afraid.

_____

The disciples were not alone in the storm. Jesus was in the boat with them. Jesus was not only with them, but Jesus was in control of the storm. Jesus heard their cry and calmed the storm. Remember WHO Jesus is. Fear makes us forget.

Jesus asked the disciples, "Why are you afraid, do you still have no faith?" Faith (trusting and believing Jesus) conquers fear. The next time you are afraid, remember that Jesus is with you. You are not alone! Jesus is God's Son. He has power over the storm. Jesus has power over everything! Jesus calmed the sea and He will calm your heart. Trust Him. He cares for you!

Do this hand motion to help remind you that faith conquers fear: Take your left hand and make it shake since fear makes us shaky. Now take your right hand and cover your left hand to make it stop shaking—this represents faith (trusting and believing Jesus). Just like your right hand covers your left hand and stops it from shaking, trusting Jesus overcomes fear.

All right! Way to go—do the hand signal and say it out loud, faith in Jesus conquers fear! Remember this hand signal to remind you and your friends you don't have to be afraid when hard and difficult things happen, you can choose to trust Jesus.

Don't forget to practice your memory verse! WHAT did Jesus say to the synagogue official? Say it out loud. Way to go!

BACK IN THE BOAT

Are you ready to go canoeing? Before we grab our oars and head to the lake, let's find out what happens another time on the Sea of Galilee. Yesterday we discovered Jesus's power over a very scary storm on the Sea of Galilee. WHAT will we find out today? Don't forget to pray!

Turn to page 224. Read Matthew 14:22-27 and mark the key words listed below.

Jesus (He) (draw a purple cross and color it yellow)

disciples (color it blue)

fear (being afraid, frightened, or terrified) (draw a black jagged circle around it)

Don't forget to mark your pronouns! And mark anything that tells you WHEN by drawing a green circle ◯ or a green clock like this: 🕐

Look at Matthew 14:22. WHAT did Jesus make the disciples do?

_____

Matthew 14:22 WHAT did Jesus do with the crowds?

_____

Matthew 14:23 WHERE did Jesus go?

_____

Matthew 14:23 WHEN is this happening?

_____

Matthew 14:23 Is anyone with Jesus on the mountain? _____

Matthew 14:24 WHERE is the boat?

_____

Matthew 14:24 WHAT is happening to the boat?

_____

Matthew 14:25 WHAT time of night is it?

_____

The fourth watch would be somewhere between 3:00 and 6:00 in the morning.

Matthew 14:25 WHAT happens?

_____

Matthew 14:26 WHAT did the disciples say when they saw Jesus walking on the sea?

_____

Matthew 14:26 HOW did they cry out?

They cried out in _____.

Draw a picture in the box below of this amazing event. Show the disciples' feelings on their faces.

Matthew 14:27 WHAT did Jesus say to the disciples?

T _ _ _ c _ _ _ _ _ _.

WHAT did Jesus mean when He said to "take courage"? To take courage in this verse means to be comforted, to be calm, to quiet your fears. HOW can the disciples be comforted and calm when they are terrified?

Matthew 14:27 WHAT did Jesus say after He said "take courage"?

"It is ___; do not _____ _____."

Jesus tells the disciples it is Him. They are not alone. Jesus is with them. The disciples don't have to be afraid. Neither do you when you are in a scary situation. Jesus is with you too! You can choose to trust Jesus.

Tomorrow you will find out WHAT happens next on the boat. Before you climb into your canoe, practice saying your memory verse.

Can you fill in the blanks of your memory verse below without looking?

"_____ _____ _____ _____

_____ _____, _____

_____." Mark 5:36

Remember Jesus's words when you feel afraid. Jesus is with you in the storm. You are not alone! He will calm your fears. Remember your hand motion for faith over fear—do it. Don't be afraid, trust Jesus!

Great work! Now climb into your canoe and have fun on the lake!

WHY ARE YOU SINKING?

"Oh, no! The canoe is filling up with water—we're sinking! Quick, scoop the water out. It's looking better…quick, paddle over to the bank so we can find out what is happening with the canoe."

Whew, that was a little scary! Now that we know our canoe is okay, let's find out WHAT happens next with Jesus and His disciples. Don't forget to pray! Thank God for helping you.

Turn to page 224. Let's read Matthew 14:28-33 and mark the key words listed below.

Jesus (Lord) (draw a purple cross and color it yellow)

Peter (color it orange)

disciples (color it blue)

fear (being afraid, frightened, or terrified) (draw a black jagged circle around it)

Don't forget to mark your pronouns! And mark anything that tells you WHEN by drawing a green circle ◯ or a green clock like this: 🕐

Ask the 5 Ws and an H questions.

Matthew 14:28 WHAT did Peter say to Jesus?

"_____, if it is _____, _____

me to _____ to _____ on the

_____."

Matthew 14:29 WHAT did Jesus say?

"_____!"

Matthew 14:29 WHAT did Peter do?

"Peter got _____ of the _____, and

_____ on the _____ and came

toward _____."

Matthew 14:30 WHAT happened when Peter walked on the water toward Jesus?

_____

Matthew 14:30 WHAT did Peter cry out?

_____

Matthew 14:31 WHAT did Jesus do?

_____

Matthew 14:31 WHAT did Jesus say to Peter?

"You of _____ _____, why did

you _____?"

Matthew 14:32 WHAT happened when they got back into the boat?

_____

Matthew 14:33 WHAT did the disciples in the boat do?

They _____ him.

To worship is to bow before God. It is to lie flat out because you recognize God is God and is to be respected. It is to acknowledge God as God. To give God the honor and praise that is due Him.

WHO did the disciples worship?

_____

WHAT did the disciples say?

_____

When the disciples saw Jesus's power over the storm and saw Him walking on water they were amazed and recognized Jesus as God's Son!

Peter was walking on the water toward Jesus. WHY did he start to sink?

_____

HOW did Peter handle being afraid?

_____

HOW did Jesus help Peter? Draw a picture in the box below to show WHAT Jesus did to help Peter when Peter cried out for Jesus to save him.

```
┌─────────────────────────────────────────────┐
│                                               │
│                                               │
│                                               │
│                                               │
│                                               │
│                                               │
└─────────────────────────────────────────────┘
```

WHAT should you do when you are afraid or terrified?

_____

Think about all the things you have learned this week at Camp Braveheart. You have learned WHO Jesus is. Jesus is God's Son.

Jesus gave His life to save you. Jesus has all power and authority, even the winds and the waves obey Jesus! Jesus calmed the storm and the disciple's hearts. Jesus told the disciples, "Take courage, it is I, do not be afraid." Now that you know all these things, when you are afraid, you can choose to...

1. **Believe**—put your trust in Jesus

2. **Take courage**—be comforted, stay calm. Jesus is with you.

3. **Cry out**—ask Jesus to help you. Jesus has ALL power and authority.

4. **Worship**—recognize WHO Jesus is, honor Him. Tell Jesus what you know about Him. Praising Jesus—reminding yourself of WHO Jesus is—will calm your fear.

When Peter was sinking, Jesus stretched out His hand and took hold of Peter. Trust Jesus. He will hold you in a storm too! Now say your memory verse out loud to a grown-up.

WHO can you trust to help you? _____

WHAT conquers fear? _____

Do you remember your hand motion? Do it!
Way to go! Faith in Jesus conquers fear!

WHAT DO YOU DO WHEN YOU ARE AFRAID?

Are you having fun at Camp Braveheart? Last week you saw how the disciples became afraid during a storm and how Peter became afraid when he was walking on water and started sinking. Even though the disciples knew Jesus and were walking with Him, they looked at their scary situations and became afraid, and their fear led to doubting Jesus.

Today we are going to look at the Old Testament to see David, a young shepherd boy that God chooses to one day become king.

HOW will this young shepherd boy handle a very hard and scary situation?

THERE'S A GIANT IN THE LAND!

YAY! Today at Camp Braveheart we are going to play capture the flag. Grab the map and mark the boundaries for Team Truth and Team Hope. All right! Both teams are in position and both flags are hidden. Let's go capture the enemy's flag!

You did it! You snuck in and evaded the enemy to capture Team Hope's flag! Grab a cold drink and some trail mix and let's get started on today's Bible adventure.

Israel has a problem. There's a giant in the land. Let's talk to God and ask Him to show you what to do when you have a giant problem that makes you afraid.

Turn to page 225. Read 1 Samuel 17:1-11 and mark the key words listed below.

Goliath (the Philistine, when it refers to Goliath) (color it brown)

Saul (color it orange)

Israel (men of Israel, ranks of Israel) (box it in blue)

battle (fight) (draw a red box around it)

dismayed (afraid) (draw a black jagged circle around it)

Don't forget to mark your pronouns! And mark anything that tells you WHERE by double underlining the WHERE in green. Mark anything that tells you WHEN by drawing a green circle ○ or a green clock like this: 🕐

Ask the 5 Ws and an H questions.

1 Samuel 17:2 WHO are Saul and the men of Israel confronting?

_____

1 Samuel 17:3 WHERE are the Philistines and Israel standing?

"The Philistines stood on the _____

on _____ _____ while Israel stood

on the _____ on the

_____ _____, with the

_____ between them."

1 Samuel 17:4 WHO is the champion who came from the armies of the Philistines?

_____

1 Samuel 17:4 HOW big was this champion?

_____

Did you know that a *cubit* was about 18 inches, and a *span* was about nine inches? That means Goliath was about 9 feet, 9 inches tall!

1 Samuel 17:5-7 HOW was Goliath dressed?

"He had a _____ _____

on his head, he was clothed with _____ –

_____ which weighed _____

_____ shekels of

_____. He also had _____

_____ on his legs and a _____

_____ slung between his shoulders.

The shaft of his _____ was like a weaver's

beam, and the _____ of his _____

weighed _____ _____

shekels of _____; his _____ –

_____ also walked _____

him."

WOW! Can you imagine WHAT this HUGE 9-foot, 9-inch tall giant wearing a bronze helmet and coat of armor weighing 5,000 shekels (which is around 125 pounds) and carrying these weapons looked like?

1 Samuel 17:8 WHAT did Goliath do?

_____

1 Samuel 17:8 WHAT did Goliath say to Israel?

"Why do you _____ _____ to draw up in

_____ _____? Am I not the

_____, and you servants of

_____? _____ a _____ for

yourselves and let him _____ _____ to _____."

1 Samuel 17:9 WHAT is Goliath's challenge to Israel?

"If he is able to _____ with me

and _____ me, then we will become

your _____; but if I

_____ against him and

_____ him, then _____ shall become our

_____ and _____ us."

1 Samuel 17:10 WHO does Goliath defy?

_____

1 Samuel 17:10 WHAT does Goliath want this man from Israel
to do?

_____

1 Samuel 17:11 WHAT happens when Saul and all Israel hear
the words of the Philistine?

_____

The word *dismayed* means to be scared, frightened, to feel pan-
icked, or intimidated, or to not know
what to do.

Draw a picture in the box below of Goliath with all his armor and weapons and King Saul and the armies of Israel. Show on their faces how Goliath, Saul, and the army of Israel felt.

HOW would you feel if you had a HUGE 9-foot, 9-inch giant terrifying you? Would you feel afraid?

_____

WHO are Saul and the men of Israel focusing on (putting their attention on)? The giant, or God?

_____

WHO should they be focusing on? A giant, who is just a man, or God?

_____

All right! You did great! Now let's discover this week's memory verse.

Take a look at the map below. Use the letter and number pair under each blank. Then go to the map and find the letter such as C at the top of the map. Then look on the left side until you find the number that goes with the C, such as 3. Find the word in the square on the map that goes with C3, and write the correct word on the blank. Do the same thing for each blank until you have discovered your verse for the week.

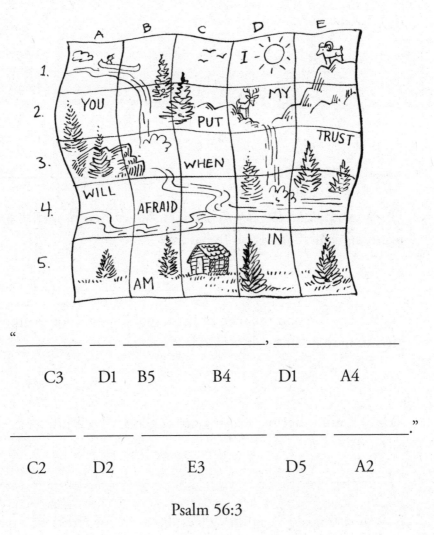

"
—————— —— ——— ————————, —— ———————
　C3　　D1　B5　　　B4　　　D1　　　A4

—————— ———— ——————— —————— ———————."
　C2　　D2　　　E3　　　　D5　　　A2

Psalm 56:3

You did it! Write this verse out on a piece of paper and practice saying it out loud three times in a row, three times today. These are David's words. WHAT will David do when He is afraid?

WHOSE ARMY ARE YOU IN?

All right Team Truth, Team Hope wants a rematch to try and capture our flag today. Are you ready to go back inside the enemy's territory to capture their flag? Before you do, let's find out what is happening with the very BIG, terrifying giant from the Philistines who wants to fight Israel—God's chosen people. If Goliath wins, Israel will become the Philistines' servants, but if Israel wins, the Philistines will serve Israel. You saw that King Saul and Israel were dismayed (scared and intimidated), very fearful of this giant. Let's find out WHAT happens next. Pray and ask God to help you understand His Word and to show you what you should do when you are in a very hard and difficult situation.

Turn to page 226. Read 1 Samuel 17:12-30 and mark the key words listed below.

God (draw a purple triangle and color it yellow)

David (color it blue)

Saul (color it orange)

Goliath (the Philistine, when it refers to Goliath) (color it brown) battle (draw a red box around it)

Israel (men of Israel) (draw a blue box around it)

afraid (draw a jagged black circle around it)

Don't forget to mark your pronouns! And mark anything that tells you WHERE by double underlining the WHERE in green. Mark anything that tells you WHEN by drawing a green circle ◯ or a green clock like this: 🕐

1 Samuel 17:12 and 17:14 WHO is David?

The y _ _ _ _ _ _ _   s _ _   of   J _ _ _ e.

1 Samuel 17:15 WHAT did David do?

_____

1 Samuel 17:16 HOW long did Goliath, the Philistine, take his stand?

_____

Can you imagine this HUGE giant coming up day after day, every morning and evening standing, and shouting at you? HOW would you feel?

1 Samuel 17:20 WHERE did David come to?

David came to the c _ _ _ _ _ of the _____.

1 Samuel 17:21 WHO drew up in battle array (formation)?

_____

1 Samuel 17:23 WHO came up from the army of the Philistines?

_____

1 Samuel 17:24 WHAT did all the men of Israel do when they saw Goliath?

_____

1 Samuel 17:26 WHAT did David say to the men about Goliath?

"For who is this uncircumcised

_____, that

he should _____ the

_____ of the

_____ _____?"

Do you know what it means to taunt someone? To taunt someone means to say mean or bad things over and over again, to make fun of them, to make them mad, to embarrass, or scare them. Goliath is taunting the armies of the living God by saying bad things over and over to shame them and make them afraid. Did it work? In verse 24 we see that the men of Israel are greatly afraid of Goliath and flee from him.

Is David afraid? _____ HOW do you know? WHAT does David say? Look back at 1 Samuel 17:26. WHOSE armies is the giant taunting?

_____

WOW! Instead of being fearful and fleeing like all the men of Israel, David—this young shepherd boy—knows Israel is the army of the living God. Israel is God's chosen people. David isn't afraid of Goliath because He knows whose army he is in. The army of the living God! David is more concerned about removing the disgrace from Israel. David's focus is on God and not on the giant. Isn't that amazing?

Tomorrow we will find out what happens next. Practice saying your memory verse out loud three times in a row, three times today! WHAT does David say he will do when he is afraid? Say it out loud!

Fantastic! HOW about you? WHAT will you do when your enemy taunts you? Will you focus on your enemy or on trusting God?

FACING YOUR GIANTS

All right, campers, today is drama day at Camp Braveheart. Are you ready to find out what happens next with David and Goliath? Pay close attention. Once we discover all the details, we are going to act it out. Talk to God and ask Him to help you face your giants today!

Now turn to page 227-228. Read 1 Samuel 17:31-47 and mark the key words listed below.

God (LORD) (draw a purple triangle and color it yellow)

David (color it blue)

Saul (color it orange)

Goliath (the Philistine, when it refers to Goliath) (color it brown)

battle (fight) (draw a red box around it)

armies (armies of Israel) (draw a blue box around it)

Let's find out what David does next. Ask the 5 Ws and an H to solve the crossword puzzle on page 57.

1 Samuel 17:32 WHAT did David tell Saul he will do?

1. (Across) "Let no man's heart fail on account of him; your servant will go and _____ with this Philistine."

1 Samuel 17:33 HOW did Saul respond?

2. (Across) "You are not able to go against this Philistine to fight with him; for you are but a youth while he has been a

_____ from his youth."

Samuel 17:34-36 WHAT did David do when he was tending his father's sheep?

3. (Across) "When a lion or a bear came and took a lamb from the flock, I went out after him and attacked him, and

_____ it from his mouth.

4. (Down) Your servant has _____ both the lion and the bear."

1 Samuel 17:36 WHY will David kill the uncircumcised Philistine?

5. (Down) The uncircumcised Philistine has

_____

6. (Across) the armies of the _____ God.

1 Samuel 17:37 WHAT did David say about the LORD?

7. (Across) "The LORD who delivered me from the paw of the lion and from the paw of the bear, He will

_____ me from the hand of this Philistine."

1 Samuel 17:38 WHAT did Saul do?

8. (Down) "Saul clothed David with his garments and put a

bronze _____ on his head, and

9. (Down) he clothed him with

_____."

1 Samuel 17:39 WHAT did David say
about the armor?

10. (Across) "I cannot go with these

because I have not _____
them."

1 Samuel 17:39 WHAT did David do?

11. (Down) He _____ them off.

1 Samuel 17:40 WHAT did David choose?

12. (Down) "He took his stick in his hand and chose for himself

five smooth _____ from the brook, and put
them in the shepherd's bag...

13. (Down) and his _____ was in his hand."

1 Samuel 17:41-43 WHAT did the Philistine say to David?

14. (Across) "Am I a dog, that you come to me with

_____?"

1 Samuel 17:44 WHAT else did the Philistine say to David?

15. (Across) "Come to me, and I will give your

_____ to the birds of the sky and the beasts of the field."

1 Samuel 17:45 HOW did David respond? HOW did David come to the Philistine?

16. (Down) "I come to you in the _____ of the

17. (Down) Lord of _____, the God of the armies of Israel, whom you have taunted."

1 Samuel 17:46 WHAT is the Lord going to do?

18. (Down) "The Lord will deliver you up into my hands, and I will strike you down and remove your _____ from you. And I will give the dead bodies of the army of the Philistines this day to the birds of the sky and the wild beasts of the earth."

1 Samuel 17:46 WHAT will all the earth know?

19. (Across) "That there is a _____ in Israel."

1 Samuel 17:47 WHAT will all this assembly know?

20. (Down) "The Lord does not deliver by _____ or by

21. (Down) _____."

1 Samuel 17:47 WHAT belongs to the Lord?

22. (Across) The _____

WOW! David is an untrained, young shepherd boy who goes into a battle with a 9-foot, 9-inch warrior giant with only five smooth stones and a sling. A giant who tells David he is going to give his flesh to the birds and the wild animals.

HOW would you feel facing this giant? Would you be afraid?

———————

WHY isn't David afraid of Goliath? WHO took care of David and rescued him from the paw of the lion and the bear when he was tending his sheep? WHO is fighting for David? **God!**

WHAT did David say to Goliath? "I come to you in the name of the LORD of hosts, the God of the armies of Israel." The name of God David calls on is "Jehovah-sabaoth" (pronounced *je-HOE-vah SAH-bah-oath*). *Jehovah* means LORD, and *sabaoth* means a mass. It refers to a mass of heavenly beings, a mass of angels, or an army of heavenly hosts.

David is calling on the LORD of Hosts, God our Deliverer. David isn't afraid of his enemy because David knows WHO God is. God's name is Jehovah-sabaoth, the LORD of hosts. David knows God is over the armies of heaven. David's eyes are fixed on God, not the giant. God is the deliverer.

WHAT else did David say? "The battle is the LORD's." You don't have to worry or be afraid when the enemy comes after you. The battle doesn't belong to you. It belongs to the LORD. God is LORD over all the armies of heaven. When all hope seems lost, when you are afraid, when you need help, when your enemy comes after you, you can run into the name of the LORD, Jehovah-sabaoth. You need to trust and depend on God. God is our deliverer. The battle is His. When you put your trust in God, He will fight for you!

Now let's act it out, Team Truth. Get a group of kids or your family and divide up into two groups, Israel and the Philistines. Pick someone to play David and someone to play Goliath and act out this amazing event. Practice your lines. WHOSE name will deliver you?

DAY FOUR

WHO WINS THE BATTLE?

You did a great job acting out the scene between David and Goliath yesterday! Today we need to find out what happens after David tells Goliath, "The battle is the LORD's and He will give you into our hands."

Talk to God. Now turn to page 229. Read 1 Samuel 17:48-58 and mark the key words listed below.

David (color it blue)

Saul, king (color it orange)

Goliath (the Philistine, when it refers to Goliath) (color it brown)

Don't forget to mark your pronouns! And mark anything that tells you WHERE by double underlining the WHERE in green.

1 Samuel 17:48 WHAT happened when Goliath, the Philistine came to meet David?

"David _____ q __ __ __ __ __ __ toward the

_____ _____ to meet the

_____."

1 Samuel 17:49 WHAT did David do?

_____

_____

1 Samuel 17:49 WHAT happened to the Philistine?

_____

1 Samuel 17:50 WHO prevailed?

_____

1 Samuel 17:50 WHAT wasn't in David's hand?

_____

1 Samuel 17:51 WHAT did David do next?

"David _____ and _____ over the Philistine

and _____ his _____ and drew it out of

its _____ and _____ him, and

_____ _____ his _____ with it."

1 Samuel 17:51 WHAT did the Philistines do when they saw
their champion was dead?

_____

1 Samuel 17:52 WHAT did Israel and Judah do?

_____

1 Samuel 17:53 WHAT did the sons of Israel do when they
returned from chasing the Philistines?

_____

1 Samuel 17:54 WHAT did David do?

"David took the _____

_____ and brought it to _____,

but he put his _____ in his _____."

1 Samuel 17:57 WHO was David brought before after he killed the Philistine?

_____

HOW did David have the courage to fight this HUGE giant who terrorized the armies of Israel?

_____

David has courage because He knows God. God had delivered David from the paw of the lion and the bear and David knew God could be depended on to protect and deliver him from the giant. David knew the battle is God's, not his. David knew God is the God who saves.

HOW about you, do you know WHO God is and WHAT He can do?

Write out one thing you know about God.

_____

Don't forget to practice your memory verse! You did great! Now act out this unbelievable scene. WHAT props do you need for David's hand?

WHO RUNS AWAY?

Today at Camp Braveheart we are going to play a trust game where you pick a buddy to help you get through an obstacle course. You will be blindfolded while your trust buddy leads you through an obstacle course without you hitting, running into, or knocking down any obstacles. The first team who gets through the course without running into any obstacles wins!

Are you ready to trust your buddy? Great! Let's go!

You did it! You trusted your buddy and didn't knock over any obstacles! All right! Now let's find out more about David's trust in God.

After David kills Goliath, David has some very hard and difficult things happen to him. King Saul brings David into his house but Saul becomes angry when he hears the women singing and dancing, saying David has killed more than Saul has. This causes King Saul to become very angry and jealous of David. He becomes so jealous that he wants to kill David.

WHAT does David do? Let's find out. Talk to God. Now look up and read 1 Samuel 21:10-12 in your Bible.

1 Samuel 21:10 WHAT did David do when he found out Saul wants to kill him?

_____

WHERE did David go?

_____

Do you know where Gath is? Gath is where David's enemy the Philistines live. Gath is Goliath's hometown. Can you believe David flees from Saul to go into the land of his enemies where they know he killed Goliath?

Look at verse 12. HOW did David feel about Achish, the king of Gath?

_____

Even though David greatly feared Achish, he ran to Gath to get away from Saul. While David is in Gath, he is seized by the Philistines. David wrote Psalm 56 during this very hard time in his life. Pull out God's Map, your Bible, and look up and read Psalm 56:1-4. Pay close attention when you read this to help you know what to do when you are afraid. Ask the 5 Ws and an H questions.

Psalm 56:1 WHO is David talking to?

_____

Psalm 56:1 WHAT does David ask God to do?

_____

Psalm 56:2 WHAT have David's foes done?

_____

Psalm 56:3 HOW does David feel?

_____

Psalm 56:3 WHAT will David do?

_____

Do you recognize David's words? It's your memory verse!

Psalm 56:4 WHAT does David say about God's word?

_____

WHERE is David's trust?

_____

WHAT does David say about man?

_____

David doesn't fear man. Even though David is in a hard situation where his enemies want to destroy him, David makes a decision to trust God.

Now look up and read Psalm 56:8-13.

Psalm 56:8 WHAT has God done?

"You have taken _____ of my

_____; _____ my

_____ in Your _____."

Psalm 56:9 WHAT will David do?

C __ __ __ on God.

Psalm 56:9 When David calls on God, WHAT will his enemies do?

_____   _____

WHY? WHO is for David? _____

Psalm 56:12 WHAT does David render to God?

_____   _____

Isn't that AWESOME? David knows WHAT to do when his enemies come after him. David knows to call on God. WHAT is this called? PRAYER! David knows when he is afraid, when he is in trouble, he can pray to God. God will hear his prayer and his enemies will turn. David knows God is for him! And even when he is afraid and in trouble, David thanks God!

WHY is David thankful? Make a list in the box on page 68. Look at WHAT David knows about God.

DAViD'S LiST ABOUT GOD

Psalm 56:8 God has taken account of David's

_____.

God p __ __ David's _____ in His

_____.

God has a b __ __ __.

Psalm 56:9 God is _____ David.

Psalm 56:10 David p __ __ __ __ es God's W __ __ d.

Psalm 56:11 David puts his _____ in God.

Psalm 56:12 God's vows are _____ on
David.

Psalm 56:13 God has _____
David's _____ from _____.

God has kept David's feet from

_____.

David was oppressed, trampled on, and afraid, so WHAT does he do? David takes his worries to God and thanks God. David knows man is only man and that God is God. Even though David is afraid, he knows God is for him and has recorded his tears in His book. David overcomes his fear by trusting God will deliver him from danger and keep him from stumbling so he can walk before God.

The next time you are afraid, ask yourself, *WHY am I afraid?* Do you know God loves and cares about you? God sees you when you are hurting, He keeps a record of your tears, and when something bad happens, He will keep you from stumbling. You can talk to God. Pray and ask Him to help you. It doesn't mean your problem or hard situation will go away. David ran from his enemies for a very long time before he was able to go home and become king. David waited and trusted God. God's plan isn't always easy, but it is always good. David thanked God. Remember God is for you! Trust Him because faith (trusting and believing God) overcomes fear. Remember your hand motion? You can also remember it like this, write the word *Faith* and under faith draw a black line and then write the word *Fear* under the black line like this:

Faith
———————
Fear

Faith over fear—you did great! Just like faith is over fear, God is over every situation in your life. Run to God. Now do the hand signal for faith over fear you learned last week.

David wrote a lot of psalms (songs) about being afraid. You could make up a song to sing when you feel afraid too. Sing to thank God and remind yourself of WHO God is. Remember, God is always good!

Now say your memory verse out loud to a grown-up.

Have a brave heart like David—think about what you have learned this week.

WHEN I am afraid, I will:

1. **Remember WHO God is.**

   Say what you know about God to yourself:

   *I know God loves me, I know God is good even when life is hard and difficult. God took care of David, God will take care of me. God is the LORD of Hosts—Deliverer. He is over all the armies of heaven, God will fight for me! I will **put my focus (my attention) on God** instead of what is making me afraid. Because I know WHO God is, **I will put my trust in Him**!*

2. **Run to God—Pray.**

   I will take my worries to God. I will pray and ask God to help me. God sees and cares about me.

3. **Give thanks.**

   I will thank God for loving and caring about me, for helping me to wait and trust Him when I am afraid.

HOW CAN YOU TRUST GOD?

Last week you saw how David handled two different scary and difficult situations in his life. As a young shepherd boy, David had the courage to fight and kill Goliath—a HUGE giant who was taunting the people of Israel, the armies of the living God.

Then, you saw David become afraid and run away because King Saul had become so jealous of David that he wanted to kill him.

HOW did David handle these scary and hard situations in his life? David made a choice to trust God. David was able to trust God because David knew WHO God is. David's faith was in God, not his circumstances.

This week we are going to learn WHO God is, WHAT He says, WHAT He is able to do, and HOW He feels about you—so when you are afraid, you will know you can trust Him too!

HiT THE TARGET—WHO iS GOD?

Good morning, Team Truth! It's time to head over to the archery field. Are you ready to see if you can hit the target at Camp Brave-heart? Great! Grab your bow and arrows and let's get started. Now stand, nock the arrow in the bowstring, draw, release, and follow through!

Wow! You did great! You had only one miss with two white hits, three black hits, and two blue hits. You came very close to gold. All right! Let's hit God's target by reading His Word. Don't forget to pray! Let's find out WHAT we can learn about God (the LORD) so we can know and trust Him like David did.

Read Psalm 103:19 printed out on page 73 and mark LORD (draw a purple triangle and color it yellow). Don't forget to mark your pronouns too!

The LORD has established His throne in the heavens,
And His sovereignty rules over all (Psalm 103:19).

Look at Psalm 103:19. WHAT do you learn about the LORD?

"The LORD has _____ His

_____ in the _____."

The LORD's "_____

_____ over _____."

WHAT does this verse show us about WHO God is and His power? God established (set up, fixed) His throne in the heavens and His sovereignty rules over all. Sovereignty is a big word that means God reigns. God is the ruler over all. That means the entire universe! God has absolute power and authority. There is nothing God doesn't have complete and total control over. Sometimes when something bad happens, you may think it doesn't look or feel like God is in control of the situation. The truth is, God is sovereign. God reigns. God is the ruler! You can trust God when you are afraid because you know WHO God is. God is in control over EVERYTHING!

HOW does God use His power and authority? Read Psalm 89:14—

> Righteousness and justice are the
> foundation of Your throne;
> Lovingkindness and truth go
> before You.

Look at Psalm 89:14. HOW does God use His power? WHAT is the foundation of God's throne?

"R __ __ __ __ __ __ __ __ __ __ __ __ and

_____ are the foundation of Your throne."

WHAT goes before God?

"_____ and

_____ go before You."

God acts in righteousness. That means God does what is right. Justice means God judges rightly—God is fair. You don't have to be afraid, because God always does what is right. Sometimes it may not look right or feel right when you are hurting or scared, but you can trust God because God always does what is right. God is always fair. Psalm 89:14 says that lovingkindness and truth go before God. Lovingkindness is God's goodness, His faithfulness, His kindness, His mercy. God is good, God is faithful to His promises. He is loving, kind, and merciful.

Let's find out more about God. Read Isaiah 14:24, 27 printed out below. Mark Lord and any pronouns for Lord like this:

Lord (draw a purple triangle and color it yellow)

Isaiah 14:24, 27

24 The Lord of hosts has sworn saying, "Surely, just as I have intended so it has happened, and just as I have planned so it will stand.

27 For the Lord of hosts has planned, and who can

frustrate it? And as for His stretched-out hand, who can turn it back?"

Look at Isaiah 14:24. WHO is God? God is the Lᴏʀᴅ of

_____.

Isaiah 14:24 WHAT happens to what God intends?

"Just as I have intended so it has _____."

Isaiah 14:24 WHAT happens to what God has planned?

It will s __ __ __ d.

Isaiah 14:27 WHAT do we see about the Lᴏʀᴅ of hosts?

"The Lᴏʀᴅ of hosts has planned, and who can

_____ it? And as for His stretched-out hand, who can _____ it _____?"

Say your answers out loud: God is the Lᴏʀᴅ of hosts, God intends it, it happens, God plans so it will stand. No one can frustrate (stop) His plan or turn back His hand! HOW amazing is that! Look at God's power!

You learned about the Lᴏʀᴅ of hosts when you learned about David going into battle with Goliath. Do you remember what this name of God means? It means God is the deliverer. God is over the armies of heaven. You can trust God when you are afraid because

God is over all the armies of heaven and the battle is His. God will fight for you! Remember, God is sovereign. He rules over all! No one can stop Him!

WHAT else can we learn about God's power? Read Isaiah 45:5-7 printed out below. Mark LORD and any pronouns for God like this:

LORD (draw a purple triangle and color it yellow)

Isaiah 45:5-7

5 I am the LORD, and there is no other;
     Besides Me there is no God.
     I will gird you, though You have not known Me;

6 That men may know from the rising to the setting of the sun
     That there is no one besides Me.
     I am the LORD, and there is no other,

7 The One forming light and creating darkness,
     Causing well-being and creating calamity;
     I am the LORD who does all these.

Isaiah 45:5 WHAT do you see about God's power?

"I am the LORD, and there is _____ _____;

besides Me there is no _____. I will _____ you."

Isaiah 45:7 "The One _____

_____ and _____

_____,

causing _____-_____ and

_____ _____;

I am the Lord who _____ all these."

Read Jeremiah 33:2-3. Mark Lord and any pronouns.

Jeremiah 33:2-3

2 Thus says the Lord who made the earth, the Lord who formed it to establish it, the Lord is His name,

3 "Call to Me and I will answer you, and I will tell you great and mighty things, which you do not know."

Look at Jeremiah 33:2. WHO is the Lord?

The Lord _____ the _____. He

_____ it to establish it.

Jeremiah 33:3 WHAT can you do?

_____ to God.

Jeremiah 33:3 WHAT will God do?

"I will _____ you, and I will _____

you _____ and _____ things, which you do not know."

WOW! Look at all you have learned about WHO God is, His

power and authority. God is the ONLY God! God will gird (equip) you. God is the One who forms light and creates darkness. It is God who made the earth—God is Creator!

God causes both well-being and calamity. A calamity is a deep trouble or misery. It can be anything that brings great loss or disaster. You might be going through a calamity right now. Did you know God is the one who causes calamities? You may not understand why God would allow this very hard and scary situation to happen, but you can trust God because God is good, loving, kind and merciful. God does what is right. God is sovereign—He rules over nations, kings, rulers, and wars. God is in control. God has a plan, and no one can frustrate it or hold back His hand. You can feel safe and secure because nothing can happen to you without God's permission. God is your deliverer! God is all-powerful. God is good ALL the time! You can call on God and He will answer you!

Now think about all you have learned about God today. Write out on the lines below, *I can trust God because I know He is*:

_____

_____

_____

AWESOME! Now that we have learned all these wonderful things about God and His power, let's discover our memory verse.

Look at the arrows in the target below. Each arrow has a number on the feather. Look at the number and find the matching blank under the target. Write the word written on each arrow on the correct blank to solve this week's verse.

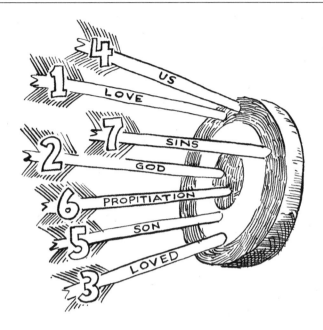

"In this is _____, not that we loved _____, but
               1   2

that He _____ _____ and sent His _____
               3   4   5

to be the _____
                           6

for our _____." 1 John 4:10
         7

Now write your verse out and practice saying it three times in a
row today! Stand, nock, draw, release, and follow through! You hit
the gold bull's-eye! Way to go!

HOW DOES GOD FEEL ABOUT YOU?

Are you ready for arts and crafts day at Camp Braveheart? We are going to have some fun and get a little messy as we learn how to make our own unique clay pot. But before we get started, let's read God's Word to find out HOW we were made. Pray and ask God to teach you!

Turn to your Observation worksheets on page 230. Read Psalm 139:1-18 and mark the key words listed below:

me (my, I, us, you—words that refers to us) (color each of these blue)

Let's ask the 5 Ws and an H questions.

Psalm 139:1 WHO knows you? _____

Psalm 139:2 WHAT does God know about you?

God knows when I _____ _____ and

when I _____ up; God understands my

_____ from afar.

Psalm 139:3 God scrutinizes my _____ and my

_____ down, God is _____

acquainted with all my _____.

Intimately acquainted means a close relationship. God knows you!

Psalm 139:4 WHAT does God know?

God knows it _____.

Psalm 139:7 Can you flee from God's

presence? _____

Psalm 139:8 WHERE is God?

"If I ascend to heaven, You are

_____; If I make my bed in

Sheol, behold, You are _____."

God is wherever you are!

Psalm 139:10 WHAT will God do?

"Your _____ will _____ me,

and Your _____ _____ will

_____ _____ of _____."

Psalm 139:12 WHAT do you see about God?

Darkness is not _____ to You.

Psalm 139:13 HOW did God make you?

"You _____ my _____ parts;

You _____ me in my _____

_____."

HOW amazing is that—YOU are made by God! You are a designer original, designed by the hand of God.

Psalm 139:14 WHAT are you to do?

_____

Psalm 139:14 HOW did God make you?

"I am _____ and

_____ made."

You are fearfully (that means awesomely) and wonderfully made by God!

Psalm 139:14 WHAT are God's works?

_____

Psalm 139:15 WHAT was not hidden from God?

_____

Psalm 139:16 WHAT did God write in His book?

_____

Psalm 139:17 WHAT are God's thoughts to you?

_____

Psalm 139:18 HOW many thoughts does God have about you?

_____

Psalm 139:18 WHO is with you?

_____

WOW! Isn't that incredible? Yesterday, when you saw that God is in control over everything, you may have wondered if God really cares about you, since He allows these scary and hard times in your life. You have just seen HOW God feels about you. God created you! God loves and cares about you! He formed you in your mother's womb! HOW AMAZING is that? God made you exactly the way He wanted you to be, you are fearfully (awesomely) and wonderfully made! God knows you! God's thoughts about you outnumber the sand! You are to give thanks to God! God loves you so very, very much! On the lines below write out a thank you note to God for HOW He created you. Write out something that is special about you.

Thank you, God, for…

_____

_____

_____

_____

God knows when you sit down and when you rise up! God knows your thoughts. God knows when you are scared. You can't flee from His presence. God knows all about you! Draw a picture in the box on the next page that shows how God is always with you.

God has written all the days of your life in His book. That means God is in control of your life. No one can touch you, hurt you, or take your life without God's permission. God has a plan for your life from the beginning to the end and no one can change His plan.

When you go through hard and difficult times, you need to remember WHO God is—the Creator. He lovingly formed and created you. He is with you and will take care of you. Even when it feels like you are alone, you are not alone—God is there, He knows your thoughts. Even when you find yourself in darkness, it is not dark to God. God sees, God cares. God is with you! Talk to God and ask Him to help you when you are afraid. God made you. God knows all your days. You are precious to Him!

Say your memory verse out loud! Tomorrow we will discover God's plan for you!

YOU ARE CHOSEN

You did an amazing job your first time at the potter's wheel! Now that your clay pot has dried and been fired, choose your favorite colors to glaze your pot to make it special, just like you are special to God!

While our pots dry, let's grab God's Map and sit by the lake to discover God's blessing for us. Don't forget to ask God for help. You know God created you, and He knows all about you. WHAT else did God do for you?

Read Ephesians 1:3-5. Mark the key words:

us (we) (color it blue)

love (draw a red heart and color it red)

Ephesians 1:3-5

3 Blessed *be* the God and Father of our Lord Jesus Christ, who has blessed us with every spiritual blessing in the heavenly *places* in Christ,

4 just as He chose us in Him before the foundation of the world, that we would be holy and blameless before Him. In love

5 He predestined us to adoption as sons through Jesus Christ to Himself, according to the kind intention of His will.

Let's ask the 5 Ws and an H questions.

Ephesians 1:3 WHO blessed us?

_____

Ephesians 1:3 HOW are we blessed? We are blessed with "every

_____   _____

in the _____   _____

in _____."

Ephesians 1:4 WHAT did God do for us?

He _____ us in Him.

Ephesians 1:4 WHEN did God choose us?

"_____ the

_____ of the

_____."

Ephesians 1:4 HOW did he choose us?

In l __ __ e.

Ephesians 1:4 WHAT are we to be?

_____ and _____ before
Him.

Ephesians 1:5 WHAT did God do for us?

"He predestined us to _____ as

_____ through _____ Christ to Himself

according to the _____ _____

of His _____."

WOW! Did you know God chose us before He created the world? HOW did God choose us? In love! God decided before the creation of the world to choose us to be adopted as sons in Christ. Let's find out more about God's plans for us. Read the verses printed below and mark the key words.

   you (yourselves, we) (color it blue)

   grace (box it in yellow and color the inside blue)

   gift (color it yellow)

Ephesians 2:8-10

8   For by grace you have been saved through faith; and that not of yourselves, *it is* the gift of God;

9   not as a result of works, so that no one may boast.

10 For we are His workmanship, created in Christ Jesus for good works, which God prepared beforehand so that we would walk in them.

Look at Ephesians 2:8. WHAT is the gift of God? HOW are you saved?

"By _____ you have been _____

_____ _____."

Ephesians 2:8 WHAT is our salvation?

It is not of yourselves, it is the _____ of God.

Ephesians 2:10 WHAT are we?

"We are His _____,
created in Christ Jesus."

Ephesians 2:10 WHAT are we created for?

_____ _____

God loves us so much that He has given us the gift of salvation! We aren't saved by the things we do. We are saved by God's grace, His gift of unearned love through faith, when we believe in Jesus. God adopts us as His child when we believe in Jesus. WHAT does it mean to believe, to put your trust in Jesus? Keep studying—we are going to find out.

Because of the great gift of salvation from God, God works in us so we can do His good works. Your life matters to God. God chose and created you with a purpose—for good works! Isn't that AWESOME?

Now, starting at page 87 look at every answer you filled in for Ephesians 1:3-5 and Ephesians 2:8-10. Find that

answer and circle it in the word search below. As you circle each word, think about WHAT God did for you, HOW much He loves you, and WHAT His purpose is for you!

C	A	D	O	P	T	I	O	N	J	D	E	V	A	S
L	H	G	I	F	T	E	H	E	A	V	E	N	L	Y
T	O	O	A	S	M	L	S	A	J	Q	D	T	I	O
Z	V	V	S	B	V	U	K	I	N	D	Q	S	G	B
I	K	J	E	E	S	K	R	O	W	H	D	I	N	Z
F	A	H	L	E	R	O	F	E	B	T	W	R	I	S
O	N	O	I	T	N	E	T	N	I	I	I	H	S	S
U	H	G	U	O	R	H	T	F	R	A	L	C	S	S
N	L	A	U	T	I	R	I	P	S	F	L	L	E	E
D	G	O	D	V	G	V	J	L	V	O	O	K	L	L
A	O	P	I	H	S	N	A	M	K	R	O	W	B	E
T	O	Q	Q	T	G	R	A	C	E	S	B	W	V	M
I	D	N	P	L	A	C	E	S	H	J	O	E	Q	A
O	H	O	L	Y	M	S	K	M	L	X	R	N	J	L
N	M	O	W	O	R	L	D	G	N	Y	C	Q	S	B

On the lines below, write out two things you learned that show God loves you.

_____

_____

All right! You did great! Say your memory verse out loud three times in a row, three times today! Tomorrow we will find out HOW God shows His love for us.

YOU ARE LOVED!

Good morning, Team Truth! Let's have breakfast before we head back to arts and crafts. Today we are going to create a heart to remind us of how God feels about us. Don't forget to pray!

Let's open God's Map to find out how God makes His love known to us. Read 1 John 4:9-10 below and mark the key words listed.

love (draw a red heart and color it red like this: ♥)

God (draw a purple triangle and color it yellow)

us (we, our) (color it blue)

Son (draw a purple cross like this: ✝ and color it yellow)

sins (color it brown)

1 John 4:9-10

9   By this the love of God was manifested in us, that God has sent His only begotten Son into the world so that we might live through Him.

10 In this is love, not that we loved God, but that He loved us and sent His Son *to be* the propitiation for our sins.

Look at 1 John 4:9. WHAT is manifested (made known) in us?

The _____ of _____.

1 John 4:9 HOW? WHAT did God do?

"God has _____ His _____ _____

_____ into the _____."

WHO is God's only begotten Son? _____

1 John 4:9 WHY did God send Jesus into the world?

"So that we might _____ _____

_____."

1 John 4:10 Did we love God or did God love us?

_____

1 John 4:10 God showed His love for us by sending His Son,
Jesus, to be WHAT for us?

The p __ __ __ __ __ __ __ __ __ __ __ for our

_____.

Because of God's great love for us, God sent His Son Jesus
into the world to be the propitiation for our sins. *Propitiation* is a
very BIG word that means when Jesus died on the cross to make

atonement for (to cover) our sins, God was satisfied with Jesus's payment for our sins.

Let's think about what we learned about Jesus in Week One, Day One on page 15. In John 1:1-2 we learned that Jesus was with God in the beginning, that Jesus is God, and that Jesus left heaven to dwell among us. Jesus became flesh by being born as a baby without sin because God is His Father. Jesus is fully God and fully man.

In John 1:29, we learned that John called Jesus "the Lamb of God who takes away the sin of the world!" Because Jesus was born without sin, and lived without sinning, He could pay for our sins. WHAT is sin? Let's see WHAT God's Word says sin is. Read James 4:17—

> Therefore, to one who knows *the* right thing to do and does not do it, to him it is sin.

Look at James 4:17. WHAT is sin?

_____

_____

Read Romans 3:23—

> For all have sinned and fall short of the glory of God.

Romans 3:23 WHO has sinned? _____

That means everyone, including you and me!

Read Isaiah 53:6—

> All of us like sheep have gone astray,
> Each of us has turned to his own way;
> But the LORD has caused the iniquity of us all
> To fall on Him.

Isaiah 53:6 HOW are we like sheep?

"All of us like sheep have _____ _____,

each of us has _____ to his

_____ _____."

That's the root of sin: turning from God's way by doing what we want to do instead of obeying God and doing what God says is right. We sin when we disobey our parents, tell a lie, or are mean to our friends. Sin is knowing the right thing to do but not doing it. God shows us that we are ALL sinners, and because God is a holy God, He must judge sin. WHAT did God do to judge sin so we wouldn't perish?

Turn to page 231. Read John 3:16-17 and mark the key words listed below.

God (draw a purple triangle and color it yellow)

loved (draw a red heart like this: and color it red)

world (draw a blue world like this: and color it blue and green)

Son (draw a purple cross like this: and color it yellow)

believes (draw a purple book like this: and color it green)

eternal life (box it in green and color it blue)

Ask the 5 Ws and an H questions.

John 3:16 WHY did God send Jesus?

_____

John 3:16 WHAT do you do to not perish?

_____

John 3:16 WHAT will you receive when you believe?

_____

John 3:17 WHY did God send Jesus into the world, to save it or judge it?

_____

John 3:17 HOW are you saved? Through _____.

Does God love you? Absolutely! He loves you so much that He gave His only begotten Son to die for your sins so you will not be judged and can live forever with Him! Jesus, who never sinned, died on the cross to take the punishment for our sins. Now, that's LOVE!

Take your hands and bend your fingers so that your knuckles and fingernails face and touch each other. As you do, make your thumbs touch each other to make a heart shape. Place your hand over your heart to remind you God loves you so much He gave His Son to save you! Tomorrow we will find out WHAT we need to believe to have eternal life and be adopted into God's family.

Before you go, practice saying your memory verse out loud three times in a row, three times today!

HOW DO YOU BECOME A CHILD OF GOD?

Wow! You did an amazing job creating and painting your pottery heart in arts and crafts. Now that the paint is dry, let's string the heart on a leather strap for you to wear as a reminder of how much God loves you.

Yesterday you discovered HOW much God loves you, WHAT sin is and HOW God sent Jesus to pay for your sins. Today, let's find out WHAT you need to believe to put your trust in Jesus and receive Jesus's unearned gift of salvation.

Don't forget to pray! Let's read 1 Corinthians 15:1-4. Mark the key words listed.

gospel (and any synonyms, like *which* and *the word*) (draw a red megaphone like this: ◀ and color it green)

Christ (He) (draw a purple cross and color it yellow)

sins (color it brown)

And mark anything that tells you WHEN by drawing a green circle ◯ or a green clock like this: 🕑

1 Corinthians 15:1-4

1   Now I make known to you, brethren, the gospel which
     I preached to you, which also you received, in which
     also you stand,

2   by which also you are saved, if you hold fast the word
     which I preached to you, unless you believed in vain.

3   For I delivered to you as of first importance what I also
     received, that Christ died for our sins according to the
     Scriptures, and that He was buried,

4   and that He was raised on the third day according to
     the Scriptures.

Look at 1 Corinthians 15:1. WHAT is the apostle Paul making
known to them?

WHAT is Paul preaching? The g __ __ __ __ __.

WHAT is the gospel? The Greek word for *gospel* is *euangelion*. It
is pronounced like this: *you-ang-ghel-ee-on.* The word *gospel* means
"good news."

1 Corinthians 15:3 WHAT is the gospel, the good news Paul
preached to them?

" _____ died for our _____ according

to the _____."

Draw a picture in the box below of Jesus dying on the cross to pay for our sins.

```
┌────────────────────────────────────┐
│                                    │
│                                    │
│                                    │
│                                    │
│                                    │
│                                    │
│                                    │
└────────────────────────────────────┘
```

The first point of the gospel is that Jesus died for our sins.

Look at 1 Corinthians 15:3. WHAT did they do with Jesus's body after He died?

_____

Did you know that after Jesus died, His body was wrapped in a clean linen cloth and buried in a tomb with a large stone against the opening of the tomb? You can read about it in Matthew 27:57-64.

Draw a picture in the box below that includes Jesus wrapped in linen buried in a garden tomb, with a big stone at the entrance of the tomb and guards guarding it.

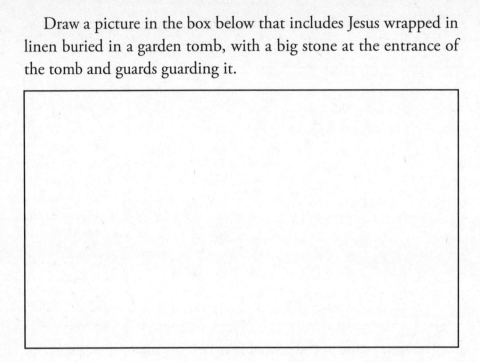

Look at 1 Corinthians 15:4. WHAT happened on the third day?

_____

In Matthew 28:1-7 when Mary Magdalene and the other Mary ran to the tomb, an angel came down from heaven, rolled away the stone, and sat on it. The guards shook with fear and the angel told Mary Magdalene and the other Mary, "Do not be afraid; for I know that you are looking for Jesus who has been crucified. He is not here, for He has risen, just as He said. Come, see the place where He was lying."

Draw a picture in the box below of the empty tomb with the stone rolled away and an angel sitting on the stone, when Jesus was resurrected from the dead.

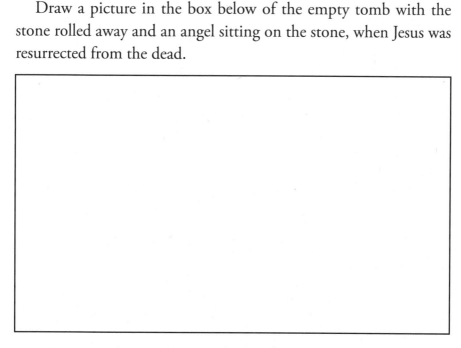

The second point of the gospel is that Jesus was buried and resurrected.

The good news of the gospel is that even though Jesus died on the cross to pay for our sins and was buried, *He didn't stay dead—* Jesus was raised on the third day! Remember what we learned yesterday: we are all sinners. We can't do anything to save ourselves, but in God's amazing love He sent Jesus to take our place and pay for our sins. We can never be good enough. Being good does not take aways our sins. Jesus is the only one who can take away sin. Look at John 14:6—

> Jesus said to him, "I am the way, and the truth, and the life; no one comes to the Father but through Me."

Look at John 14:6 WHO is Jesus?

Jesus is the _____, the _____ and the

_____.

John 14:6 WHAT is the ONLY way to the Father?

_____

Jesus is the ONLY way to God. We can believe Jesus because He
is the truth. When we believe in Jesus, we receive eternal life.
Look at John 1:12—

> But as many as received Him, to them He gave the
> right to become children of God, *even* to those who
> believe in His name.

John 1:12 WHAT happens when you receive Jesus by believing
in His name?

He gives us the right to become _____

of _____!

So, HOW do you become God's child? HOW do you put your
trust in Jesus Christ and receive eternal life?

The first thing you need to do is know WHO Jesus is. You have
to:

- believe that Jesus is God's Son
- believe Jesus is God

- understand that when Jesus lived as a man, He lived a perfect life without sinning

- believe Jesus died on a cross to pay for our sins

- believe Jesus was buried, and God raised Him from the dead three days later

- believe that you are a sinner and that you need Jesus to save you because you can't save yourself

- confess to God that you are a sinner and tell Him you want to turn away (repent) from sin

- be willing to turn away from doing things your way and start obeying Jesus. You have to turn your entire life over to God to become a follower of Jesus Christ and let Jesus have complete control over your life.

If you truly believe in WHO Jesus is and WHAT He did for you, and you know you are a sinner and cannot save yourself, ask: *Am I ready to give my life to Jesus and let Him take over my life?*

It's a BIG decision. If you are ready, ask a grown-up to help you. Once you give your life to Jesus, your sins will be forgiven and you will become a child of God. You will live forever with God and Jesus!

Look at what else you will receive. Read Ephesians 1:13-14 printed out on the next page. Mark the key words listed.

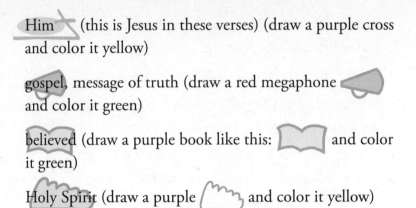

Him (this is Jesus in these verses) (draw a purple cross and color it yellow)

gospel, message of truth (draw a red megaphone and color it green)

believed (draw a purple book like this: and color it green)

Holy Spirit (draw a purple and color it yellow)

Ephesians 1:13-14

13 In Him, you also, after listening to the message of truth, the gospel of your salvation—having also believed, you were sealed in Him with the Holy Spirit of promise,

14 who is given as a pledge of our inheritance, with a view to the redemption of God's *own* possession, to the praise of His glory.

Look at Ephesians 1:13. WHO are you sealed with, in Jesus, after you listen to the gospel, the message of truth, and believe in Jesus?

_____

Ephesians 1:14 WHAT is the Holy Spirit a pledge of?

_____

Look at John 14:16-17, 26 printed out on the next page. Mark the key word. Don't forget your pronouns! This is Jesus speaking.

Holy Spirit (Helper, Spirit of Truth) (draw a purple
and color it yellow)

John 14:16-17, 26

16 I will ask the Father, and He will give you another
Helper, that He may be with you forever;

17 *that is* the Spirit of truth, whom the world cannot
receive, because it does not see Him or know Him, *but*
you know Him because He abides with you and will
be in you.

26 But the Helper, the Holy Spirit, whom the Father will
send in My name, He will teach you all things, and
bring to your remembrance all that I said to you.

Look at John 16:16. WHAT will the Father give you?

Another _____

John 16:17 WHERE will the Holy Spirit live?

"He _____ with you and will be

_____ _____."

The word *abide* means to dwell with. The Holy Spirit will live in
you!

John 14:26 WHAT will the Holy Spirit do?

_____

Isn't that AWESOME? God's Spirit comes to live inside of you
when you receive Jesus Christ as your Sav-
ior! Your body becomes His home. The
Holy Spirit is your Helper. He will be your
teacher and teach you all things. The
Holy Spirit is given as a promise of your
inheritance. He is the guarantee that you
are going to heaven and that you have eternal life!

Read Acts 1:8 and mark the key words
listed.

Holy Spirit (draw a purple ⌒ and color it yellow)

power (draw a red stick of dynamite like this: ⬭)

Acts 1:8

8 But you will receive power when the Holy Spirit has
come upon you; and you shall be My witnesses both in
Jerusalem, and in all Judea and Samaria, and even to
the remotest part of the earth.

Acts 1:8 WHAT will you receive when the Holy Spirit comes
on you?

P __ __ __ __!

Once you believe in Jesus and receive the Holy Spirit you will
have God's power! It's God's Spirit living in you that gives you the
power to walk in God's ways. You just can't do it without God's

Spirit, but with God's Spirit you can live your new life in Him. Isn't that amazing? Once you become God's child, you will receive God's power to live inside of you. You never have to be afraid or feel alone, because God's Spirit will live inside of you!

Think about all the things you have learned this week.

WHEN you are afraid, you can trust God because you know:

1. **WHO God is—God is sovereign; He is in control.** God rules over nations, kings, rulers, and wars. All power and authority belong to Him. God always does what is right. Lovingkindness and truth go before God. God is good, He is faithful to His promises, and He is loving, kind, and merciful.

2. **HOW God feels about you—God created you and loves you!** God wove you in your mother's womb, you are fearfully and wonderfully made by the hand of God. God has written all the days of your life in His book. He sees you, and He knows you.

3. **God has a plan for your life from the beginning to the end and no one can change His plan.**

4. **God chose you before He created the world.** God sent His Son from heaven to die on a cross to save you from sin. Jesus chose to give His life to save you. If you believe and trust in who Jesus is and what He did to save you, if you confess and ask God to forgive your sins, and if you turn your life over to God and Jesus, then you are adopted as God's child. You are blessed, chosen, loved, forgiven, known, and redeemed. You have God's grace, your life has a purpose, and you are created for good works that God has planned just for you!

5. **God has an inheritance for His children.** When you become God's child, God gives you the gift of the Holy Spirit living inside of you. The Holy Spirit will give you God's power to walk in God's ways. God has a home for you in heaven where you can live with God and Jesus forever! WOW! How AMAZING is that?

Now say your memory verse out loud to a grown-up. Look at HOW much God loves you! God gave His Son to save you! God has BIG plans for you! Because of God's great love, mercy, and power, you can trust Him to help you when you are afraid. Sing a song or write a note to God on the lines below to say thank you to God for all He has done for you.

Thank You, God, for…

_____

_____

_____

_____

_____

WHO SHOULD YOU FEAR?

You are learning so much at Camp Braveheart! You have learned WHO Jesus is and have seen His awesome power when He calmed the storm and the disciples' fears. You have seen Jesus's awesome love and compassion as He reached down to help Peter when he was sinking, and when He gave His life to save yours.

You have learned that when you are afraid, you are to believe—put your trust in Jesus and cry out to Him. Faith (believing and trusting Jesus) conquers fear. (Can you do the hand signal for faith over fear?)

You have also seen how David trusted God instead of being afraid of the giant. Even as a young boy, David knew WHO God is, which gave him the courage to stand and fight Goliath. David knew God is the Deliverer. In Psalm 56, we saw that when David was afraid he put his trust in God, he called on God, and thanked God.

You have learned WHO God is. You know God is sovereign. He rules over everything both good and bad with power, authority, righteousness (doing the right thing), love, kindness, and mercy. God loves you! He chose you, created you, knows you, forgives you, adopts you, and plans all your days. God loves you so much that He sent His only Son, Jesus, to die to save you from your sins and make you part of His family! HOW AWESOME is that?

You have been learning WHO you can trust, WHAT you should do when you are afraid, and HOW much God and Jesus love you. This week we are going to find out WHO we are to fear and WHY.

WHAT IS THE FEAR OF THE LORD?

Good morning, Team Truth! Today at Camp Braveheart we get to go fishing!

Grab God's Map—your Bible—your fishing rod, and a picnic lunch, and head to the lake. Let's sit on the bank. Before we fish for our dinner, let's fish for truth. Let's read God's Word to find out WHO we are to fear and WHY. Pray and ask God to teach you as you discover what His Word says.

Read Proverbs 9:10 and mark the key phrase and key words listed.

the fear of the LORD (draw a black jagged circle around it)

wisdom (box it in orange and color it yellow)

knowledge (color it green)

The fear of the LORD is the beginning of wisdom, and the knowledge of the Holy One is understanding (Proverbs 9:10).

Look at Proverbs 9:10. WHAT is the beginning of wisdom?

_____

WHAT does the *fear of the* LORD mean? Does it mean we are to be afraid of God? No, it doesn't. The fear of the Lord is to know God, to respect God, to be in awe of God, and to reverence Him. To fear God means to listen and obey Him.

When we fear God by treating Him with honor and respect, when we listen to and obey Him, it is the beginning of wisdom. Wisdom is having good judgment and understanding how to live. Wisdom is knowing, "This is what God says, this is truth, so this is what I will do." Knowledge is knowing facts and truth, and wisdom is understanding and living out God's truth.

So, HOW do we learn the fear of the Lord? WHAT teaches us how to fear God—to treat Him with honor and respect, to listen and obey Him? WHAT will give us knowledge and wisdom? Read Deuteronomy 17:14, 18-20 and mark the key words listed below:

the law (it, commandments) (draw black tablets around it like this:)

fear the LORD (draw a black jagged circle around it)

Mark anything that tells you WHEN with a green circle ○ or a green clock like this: 🕐

Deuteronomy 17:14, 18-20

14 When you enter the land which the LORD your God gives you, and you possess it and live in it, and you say, "I will set a king over me like all the nations who are around me"

18 Now it shall come about when he sits on the throne of his kingdom, he shall write for himself a copy of this law on a scroll in the presence of the Levitical priests.

19 It shall be with him and he shall read it all the days of his life, that he may learn to fear the LORD his God, by carefully observing all the words of this law and these statutes,

20 that his heart may not be lifted up above his countrymen and that he may not turn aside from the

commandment, to the right or the left, so that he and his sons may continue long in his kingdom in the midst of Israel.

Look at Deuteronomy 17:18. WHAT is the king to do?

_____

Deuteronomy 17:19 WHAT is the king to do with this copy of the law?

"It shall be _____ him and he shall _____

it...carefully _____ _____

the _____ of this _____ and these statutes."

Deuteronomy 17:19 WHY is the king to read it? WHAT will reading and carefully observing the copy of the law do?

"That he may _____ to _____ the

_____ his _____."

Deuteronomy 17:19 HOW often is the king to read it?

_____

Deuteronomy 17:20 HOW will this help the king?

So "that his _____may not be

_____ _____ above his countrymen

and that he may not _____ _____

from the _____, to the

_____ or to the _____."

Deuteronomy 17:20 WHAT will happen if the king does this?

_____

Great work! God told Moses the king was to write a copy of the law. The *law* is the Torah, the first five books of the Bible: Genesis, Exodus, Leviticus, Numbers, and Deuteronomy. The king was to write a copy of the law in front of the priests and read it all the days of his life so the king could learn the fear of the Lord. The fear of the Lord comes from knowing and carefully observing God's laws and statues. God's Word is truth. It will help you to be careful to not turn to the left or to the right but to stay on God's path, listening to and obeying God.

Now throw your fishing line into the lake to discover your memory verse this week. Look at all the fish in the lake below. Each one has a number on it. Catch each fish and place the word that is written in its air bubble on the blank with the number of that fish written underneath.

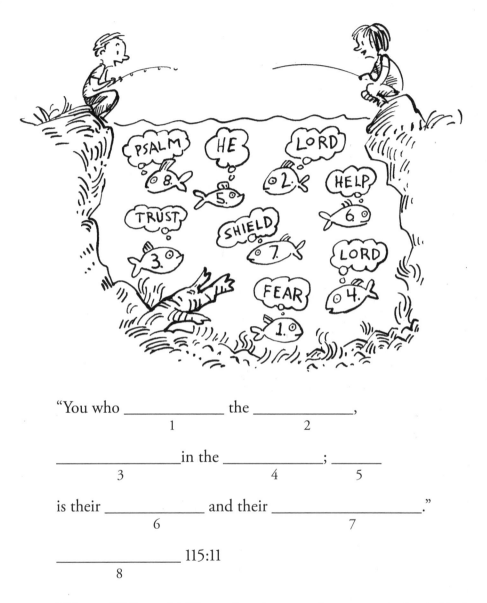

"You who _____ the _____,
              1   2

_____in the _____; _____
        3   4   5

is their _____ and their _____."
           6   7

_____ 115:11
     8

What a BIG catch! If you fear (respect, honor, and obey) God, then God is your help and your shield! Write your memory verse out on a piece of paper and practice saying it three times in a row, three times every day!

Do You Fear God or Man?

All right, Team Truth! Yesterday we went fishing for truth and we reeled in a BIG catch as we looked at Proverbs 9 and Deuteronomy 17 to learn about the fear of the Lord.

In Deuteronomy 17, we saw that the king was to copy, read, and carefully observe the law and its statues so he would learn the fear of the Lord and know how to walk all the days of his life. Today, let's look at Deuteronomy 31 to see WHAT else we can learn about the fear the Lord.

Talk to God. Read Deuteronomy 31:10-12 printed out below. Mark the key words listed.

the law (it, commandments) (draw black tablets around it like this: ⬜⬜)

fear the LORD (draw a black jagged circle around it)

Mark anything that tells you WHEN by drawing a green circle ⭕ or a green clock like this: 🕐

Deuteronomy 31:10-12

10 Then, Moses commanded them, saying, "At the end of *every* seven years, at the time of the year of remission of debts, at the Feast of Booths,

11 when all Israel comes to appear before the LORD your God at the place which He will choose, you shall read this law in front of all Israel in their hearing.

12 Assemble the people, the men, and the women and children and the alien who is in your town, so that they may hear and learn and fear the LORD your God, and be careful to observe all the words of this law."

Look at Deuteronomy 31:11. WHAT did Moses command them to do when all of Israel appears before the Lord?

_____

Deuteronomy 31:12 WHO is to be assembled there?

"the _____, the _____ and the

_____ and _____ and the

_____ who is in your town."

Deuteronomy 31:12 WHAT are all the people to hear and learn?

_____

Deuteronomy 31:12 HOW? WHAT are they to be careful to do?

_____

Did you notice kids, just like you, were included to hear and learn the fear of the Lord? So, HOW do we learn to fear the Lord?

_____

God thinks it's important for you as a child to hear and to learn the fear of the Lord, to be careful to observe all His words. You are learning HOW right now by studying and learning God's Word!

You have seen in Deuteronomy 17 and 31 that learning to fear the Lord, reverencing, respecting, and honoring God comes from knowing God's Word. It's not just knowing God's Word but obeying God by doing what He says is right.

Will you choose to do to what God says? _____

The fear of the Lord will keep you from turning to the left or the right, it will keep you on God's path. God wants EVERYONE, our leaders, men, women, children, and aliens (those who are from other places), to know and understand the fear of the Lord. When you learn the fear of the Lord by respecting God as God, and you do what God says, that is how you overcome all other fears.

Let's read Proverbs 29:25 below. Mark these key words:

fear (draw a black jagged circle around it)

man (color it orange)

trusts (draw a blue T over the word)

Lord (draw a purple triangle and color it yellow)

Proverbs 29:25

25 The fear of man brings a snare, but he who trusts in the Lord will be exalted

Look at Proverbs 29:25. WHAT two things are contrasted? A contrast shows how two things are different or opposite, such as light and dark, or truth and lies. WHAT two things are opposite in Proverbs 29:25?

F __ __ __ and t __ __ __ __

When you fear man, WHAT does it bring?

A _____

A snare is a trap. When you fear (tremble) because of man, you are trapped and your actions are controlled by fear.

Proverbs 29:25 WHAT happens when you trust in the Lord?

You will be _____.

Exalted means to be lifted up—secure. When you trust God instead of being afraid, you will be secure.

Isn't that awesome? You are secure when you fear God, but if you fear man you are caught in a trap! Have you ever feared that if you didn't do what other kids are doing you would be left out and made fun of? That's exactly what it means to fear man—your behavior is controlled by your fear of another person.

You have a choice: you can fear God or fear man. When you choose to fear God (honoring God and doing what He says is right) you will be able to have self-control rather than panic in the face of all other fears. Remember how David had the courage to stand and fight when he faced Goliath? David's behavior was controlled by his fear of God, the Lord of Hosts. David knew God. He chose to trust and honor God, not to fear man.

When you know WHO God is, when you believe He has all power, control, and authority, and when you understand how much He loves you, then you will be able to trust Him even when you don't understand what is happening and you feel scared.

WHAT will you do? Will you keep studying God's Word so you can learn WHO God is and how to live to honor Him? Will you obey, do what God says is right? WHO will you fear: God or man? Write out what you will do.

_____

Remember, when you fear God, you will be exalted, lifted up, and secure! Think about your memory verse. Can you fill in the blanks below without looking?

You who _____ the _____,

_____in the _____; He is their

_____ and their _____. Psalm 115:11

AWESOME! Now say your verse out loud with a strong, confident voice! WHO is the Lord?

WHO iS FOR YOU?

Good morning, Team Truth! Let's head back to the lake to see if we can reel in another BIG catch for Camp Braveheart's big fish fry tonight. Let's talk to God and ask Him to help us.

Read Psalm 118:4-9 and mark the key words listed.

fear (draw a black jagged circle around it)

my (I, me) (color it blue)

LORD (draw a purple triangle and color it yellow)

trust (refuge) (draw a blue T over the word)

Psalm 118:4-9

4 Oh let those who fear the LORD say, "His lovingkindness is everlasting."

5   From *my* distress I called upon the LORD; the LORD answered me *and set me* in a large place.

6   The LORD is for me; I will not fear; what can man do to me?

7   The LORD is for me among those who help me; therefore I will look *with satisfaction* on those who hate me.

8   It is better to take refuge in the LORD than to trust in man.

9   It is better to take refuge in the LORD than to trust in princes.

Look at Psalm 118:4. WHAT can those who fear the Lord say?

_____

Psalm 118:5 WHAT can those who fear the Lord do when they are in distress?

_____

Psalm 118:5 WHAT will God do?

_____

Psalm 118:6 WHO is for you?

_____

Psalm 118:6 Since God is for you, WHAT aren't you to do?

_____

Psalm 118:6 WHY aren't you to fear man?

"What can _____ _____ to _____?"

Psalm 118:7 WHAT will the LORD do for you?

_____

Psalm 118:8 WHAT is better?

_____

"Princes" in verse 9 means rulers, which would be your leaders.

WHO do you think people trust more, their leaders or God?

_____

WHO should you trust and respect more? WHO is in control?

_____

Look at what we just learned! God's lovingkindness is ever-lasting. When we are distressed, we can call on Him and He will answer us. We don't have to be afraid of man, man is not in control. God is! We aren't to be afraid of what others might do. We are to trust God. God will deliver us.

Read Psalm 115:9-11. Mark the key words listed:

LORD (draw a purple triangle and color it yellow)

trust (draw a blue T over the word)

fear (draw a black jagged circle around it)

Psalm 115:9-11

9 O Israel, trust in the LORD; He is their help and their shield.

10 O house of Aaron, trust in the LORD; He is their help and their shield.

11 You who fear the LORD, trust in the LORD; He is their help and their shield.

Look at Psalm 115:11. WHO is the Lord to those who fear and trust Him?

_____

Look back at Psalm 115:9-11. Underline and write a number over every place God repeats "trust in the LORD, He is their help and their shield" to count HOW many times God says it. HOW many times did you count?

_____ times

God repeats this phrase to Israel, Aaron, and those who fear Him three times because it is important. WHAT can man do to us? God is in control. God is our helper and defender! HOW amazing is that?

So, WHAT should you do when you are afraid?

When I am I afraid, I will put my _____ in God.

God is my _____ and my _____!

Now practice your memory verse, say it three times in a row, three times today! Tomorrow we will meet a king to find out HOW this king responds to the threats of man.

WHO IS AFRAID?

Way to go, Team Truth! You reeled in the most fish for our big fish fry! Did you enjoy cooking your fish over an open fire? They tasted so good. Are you ready to look at God's Map to find out HOW a king responds to the threats of man? Great! Let's talk to God. Let's find out WHO this king is and WHAT he does when he is threatened by man.

Turn to page 231. Read 2 Chronicles 20:1-12 and mark the key words listed below. Don't forget your pronouns!

Jehoshaphat (color it blue)

The Lord (draw a purple triangle and color it yellow)

afraid (draw a black jagged circle around it)

cry (draw a red C around it like this: C)

hear (draw a green ear like this: ꓵ)

deliver (draw a blue circle and color it red)

Mark anything that tells you WHEN by drawing a green circle

◯ or a green clock like this: ⏱. Answer the 5 Ws and an H questions.

> 2 Chronicles 20:1 WHAT did the sons of Moab, the sons of Amnon, and some of the Meunites come to do to Jehoshaphat?

_____

> 2 Chronicles 20:3 HOW did Jehoshaphat feel?

_____

Was that a normal emotion to have in this situation?

_____

> 2 Chronicles 20:3 WHAT did Jehoshaphat do?

He _____ his

_____ to seek the _____,

and proclaimed a _____ throughout all of

_____.

WOW! Did you notice the first thing Jehoshaphat did when he was afraid? He turned his attention to seek the Lord.

> 2 Chronicles 20:4 WHAT did Judah do?

_____

2 Chronicles 20:5 WHERE is Jehoshaphat?

_____

2 Chronicles 20:6 WHO is Jehoshaphat talk-

ing to? _____

WHAT is this called?

P __ __ __ __ __.

Jehoshaphat is praying to God. Look at how Jehoshaphat begins his prayer. Jehoshaphat starts by worshipping God.

HOW does Jehoshaphat worship God? Look at WHAT Jehoshaphat says about God in verses 6-12. HOW does Jehoshaphat describe God?

2 Chronicles 20:6 God of our _____

God in the _____

R __ __ __ __ over all the _____ of

the _____

P __ __ __ __ and _____ are in Your

_____.

No _____ can _____ against You.

2 Chronicles 20:7 God, _____ out the inhabitants
of this land.

G __ __ __ the land to the _____

of Abraham. God is Abraham's f __ __ __ __ __ forever.

2 Chronicles 20:9 We c __ __ to _____ in our

_____, and You will _____

and _____ us.

2 Chronicles 20:12 God, will You not _____
them?

Our _____ are on You.

Isn't this amazing? When King Jehoshaphat was afraid, the first
thing he did was turn his attention to seek God. He put His eyes on
God! He called for a fast. A fast is when you go without drinking
or eating. Jehoshaphat knows that when there is no hope, such as
when the enemy is coming against them, there is a God in heaven
who is in control of everything! Like Jehoshaphat, all God's people can humble themselves before God by fasting, seeking God's
presence, and asking for His help. God is the only one who has the
power to change things. When we are afraid or without hope, we
can run to God because God loves us!

Jehoshaphat starts his prayer by praising God, saying what he knows about WHO God is and WHAT God can do. Jehoshaphat knows God is the ruler over all the kingdoms and nations. He knows God has the power to drive out the inhabitants of this land. He tells God of their distress and powerlessness before a great multitude. He says "nor do we know what to do, but our eyes are on You" (2 Chronicles 20:12).

WHAT trust! Isn't that amazing? Jehoshaphat's eyes and attention are not on the enemy or the situation. Jehoshaphat's eyes are on God! WHERE do you look when you are afraid? Do you look at what is happening (the bad situation), or do you look to God?

WHAT can you do when you are in a bad or hard situation and you don't know what to do?

_____

Do you believe God can help you when it looks like there is no

hope?_____

WHY do or WHY don't you believe God will help you?

_____

The next time you are afraid, go to God like Jehoshaphat did. Look up at heaven. Tell God, "You are God in the heavens, You are the Ruler over all the kingdoms of the nations. Power and might are in Your hand. No one can stand against You." Then tell God why you are afraid. Tell Him, "I am powerless, I don't know what to do, but my eyes are on You." Tell God, "I trust You to help and take care of me. You love me. You are in control. You are good. I trust You will do what is right for me in this situation. You are for me!" Thank God for helping, loving, and taking care of you.

WHEN we look to God and praise Him for WHO He is, it will calm our fears and put peace in our hearts. That's why it is so important to know God's Word. Remember the next time you are afraid, STOP—look up at heaven and tell God, "I don't know what to do, my eyes are on You!"

Practice saying your memory verse out loud, three times in a row, three times today! WHO is your help and your shield? Say it out loud!

Way to go! Tomorrow we will find out WHAT happens next to King Jehoshaphat and God's people.

Do not Fear—the Lord is with you

Rise and Shine, Team Truth! Hurry up, Cook is making homemade doughnuts this morning! Yum! Those doughnuts are the BEST! Wipe the sugar off your fingers so you can find out WHAT happens after King Jehoshaphat turned his attention to seek God.

Turn to page 232. Read 2 Chronicles 20:13-30 and mark the key words listed. Don't forget your pronouns!

> Jehoshaphat (color it blue)
>
> The Lord (draw a purple triangle and color it yellow)
>
> fear (dismayed) (draw a black jagged circle around it)
>
> trust (draw a blue T over it)

Mark anything that tells you WHEN by drawing a green circle ◯ or a green clock like this: 🕐. Ask the 5 Ws and an H questions.

2 Chronicles 20:13 WHAT was all of Judah doing?

_____

2 Chronicles 20:14 WHAT happened in the midst of the assembly?

_____

2 Chronicles 20:15 WHAT did the Spirit of the Lord say to all of Judah, the inhabitants of Jerusalem, and King Jehoshaphat?

"Do not _____ or be _____

because of this great _____."

2 Chronicles 20:15 WHOSE battle is it?

_____

2 Chronicles 20:16 WHAT are they to do tomorrow?

"Tomorrow _____ down _____ them."

2 Chronicles 20:17 WHAT does the Spirit of the Lord tell them about the battle?

_____

_____

2 Chronicles 20:17 WHAT are they to do?

"_____ yourselves, _____

and see the _____ of the

_____ on your _____, O Judah and
Jerusalem.

"Do _____ _____ or be

_____; tomorrow go out

to _____ them, for the _____ is

_____ _____."

AWESOME! God is going to fight the battle for them! They just
have to stand, watch, and trust God. The battle is the Lord's! When
we learned about David and Goliath, do you remember the name
of God that was used? God's name is "Jehovah-saboath," the Lord
of Hosts. God is over the angel armies in heaven. The Lord of Hosts
will fight for you! When all hope is lost, God is the Deliverer. God
will deliver you!

Look at 2 Chronicles 20:18. WHAT did Jehoshaphat do?

_____

2 Chronicles 20:18 WHAT did all of Judah and the inhabitants
of Jerusalem do?

_____

2 Chronicles 20:19 WHAT did the Levites do?

_____

Do you remember what it means to worship? To worship is to
bow before God. It is to make yourself low before God because you

recognize He is to be respected. It is to acknowledge God as God—
to give God the honor and praise that is due Him.

   2 Chronicles 20:20 WHAT did King Jehoshaphat tell them to
   do?

P __ __ your _____ in the _____ your

_____ and you will be _____.

To be established means to be supported, to stand firm.

   2 Chronicles 20:21 WHAT did those he appointed sing to the
   Lord as they went out before the army?

"G __ __ __ _____ to the _____,

for His _____ is

_____."

Look at how they went out to battle with singing and praise!

2 Chronicles 20:22 WHAT happened? WHAT did the Lord set against the sons of Ammon, Moab, and Mount Seir?

A __ __ __ __ __ __ __

An ambush is a surprise attack.

2 Chronicles 20:23 WHAT happened to the sons of Ammon, Moab, and Mount Seir when God set ambushes against them? WHO did they help destroy?

_____

2 Chronicles 20:24 Did anyone escape? _____

When they went out to battle singing and praising God, God set ambushes against Ammon, Moab, and Mount Seir. They were so surprised and confused that they turned on one another and destroyed each other.

2 Chronicles 20:25 HOW many days did it take them to take the spoil?

_____

WHY did it take so long?

_____

2 Chronicles 20:26 WHAT did they do on the fourth day?

They b __ __ __ __ __ d the Lord.

2 Chronicles 20:27 HOW did they return to Jerusalem?

With ___ ___ __! WHY? WHAT did the Lord do?

The Lord made them _____ over their

_____.

2 Chronicles 20:30 WHAT did you see about the kingdom of Jehoshaphat?

_____

WHY? Because _____ gave him _____ on

_____ _____.

WOW! Look at all God did! Jehoshaphat and all of Judah put their eyes on God, they humbled themselves by fasting and worshipping God. They asked for God's help, and God delivered them! The battle is the Lord's. All they had to do was stand and see, to do what God told them to do. Because they put their trust in God, they returned home with joy and God gave them rest on every side!

Draw a picture in the box below. Show what Jehoshaphat did when he was afraid. Then, show how they returned home in victory with joy!

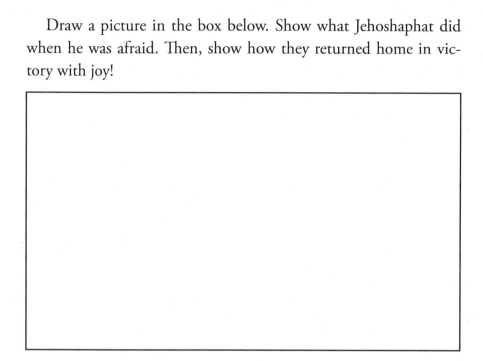

Jehoshaphat had faith. He trusted God. He ran to God for help. He praised and worshipped God. Do your hand signal for faith over fear. Do you have faith? Will you put your trust in God like King Jehoshaphat did? WHAT will you do when you are afraid and your enemy comes after you? Think about all you have learned. Jehoshaphat feared (reverenced and obeyed) God instead of being afraid of man. He knew WHO God is. He asked God what to do. He worshipped God. He trusted God. And he thanked God.

HOW about you? Will you remind yourself of WHO God is, WHAT He has done for you—and respond with praise and worship? Will you ask Him to help you and thank Him for hearing your prayer and answering the next time you are afraid?

Do you fear God or man? Remember God is the one WHO gives you victory and joy! Say your memory verse out loud to a grown-up. Fantastic! Sing a song to worship God today!

Now think about all you learned this week. **WHAT should you do when you are afraid?**

1. **Fear God**—To fear God is to know, respect, and honor God. If you fear God, then you will listen to and obey Him. When you fear God, you will be lifted up and secure. Remind yourself of this by saying, "God will help me overcome my fears. I will put my trust in God. God is my help and my shield."

2. **Don't fear man**—When you fear man instead of God, you are caught in a trap because your behavior is controlled by fear of another person. What can man do to you? God is in control.

3. **Look to God and pray**—Turn your attention to God like King Jehoshaphat did. Humble yourself before God and worship Him. Tell God you don't know what to do but your eyes are on Him. Ask God to help you.

4. **Obey**—Do what God tells you to do. The children of Israel went down to the enemy singing and praising God. God said not to fear or be dismayed because the Lord is with you! Remember the battle is the Lord's and He will fight for you! God ambushed Jehoshaphat's enemies, and He will take care of you too.

5. **Give thanks**—They returned to Jerusalem in victory with joy! God gave them rest on all sides! Thank God for giving us victory and joy!

HOW CAN YOU BE STRONG
AND COURAGEOUS?

Last week was a great week at Camp Braveheart as we learned something very important—the fear of the Lord. We discovered that fearing God means we are to honor and respect God as God. Fearing God is to trust God and do what God says. God's Word, the Bible, teaches us to fear God. Fearing God is the beginning of wisdom and knowledge, which helps us understand and live out what God says. Fearing God helps us not to panic and gives us peace, because when we fear man, we are caught in a trap!

We saw King Jehoshaphat choose to fear God by seeking God,

putting his eyes on God, and worshipping and obeying God instead of being afraid of man. And we saw how God delivered him and the children of Israel. All they had to do was to trust God and obey—do what God told them to do—and they returned home in victory and joy!

This week we will discover WHAT God tells Joshua to do, WHO our enemy is, HOW God has equipped us, and HOW we can have peace when our hearts are troubled. Are you ready to find out what God says about how to have a brave heart even when you are afraid?

FASTEN ON TO GOD

Good morning, Team Truth! Are you ready for a new adventure? Today we are going to head out on the trail with Team Hope to hike through the forest for an awesome rock-climbing adventure. Let's pack our gear and talk to God as we get ready for a BIG challenge to climb Mount Triumph.

We're here. WOW! Look at that mountain. Do you feel a little nervous? Before we begin our climb, let's talk to God and ask Him to help us have a brave heart. All right! Now we are ready.

Today we are going to open our Map (God's Word) to the book of Joshua. After Moses died, God chose Joshua to take the sons of Israel into the promised land. Let's find out WHAT God tells

Joshua that gives him the confidence to lead the children of Israel into the promised land filled with their enemies.

Turn to page 234. Read Joshua 1:1-9 and mark the key words listed below.

Lord (God) (draw a purple triangle and color it yellow)

Joshua (color it blue)

the law (book of the law) (draw black tablets around it like this:)

do not tremble or be dismayed (draw a black jagged circle around it)

be strong and courageous (draw a green box around it)

Don't forget to mark your pronouns! Mark anything that tells you WHEN by drawing a green circle ◯ or a green clock like this: 🕐. Answer the 5 Ws and an H questions.

Joshua 1:1 WHO spoke to Joshua?

_____

Joshua 1:2 WHAT did the Lord tell Joshua to do?

"Arise, _____ this _____, you

and all this people, to the _____ which I am giving to them."

Joshua 1:2 WHO is God giving the land? _____

Joshua 1:5 WHAT does God say to Joshua that would give him confidence to go in and take the land that God had promised the sons of Israel?

"No _____ will *be able* to _____ before

_____ all the _____ of your _____.

Just as I have been _____ Moses, I will be

_____ _____; I will not _____ you or

_____ you."

Joshua 1:6 WHAT does God tell Joshua to do?

_____

Joshua 1:6 WHAT did God swear (promise) to give their fathers?

_____

Joshua 1:7 WHAT did God tell Joshua to be careful to do?

"Be careful to do according to all the _____."

Joshua 1:7 HOW were they to do according to the law?

"Do _____ _____ from _____ to the

_____ or to the _____."

Joshua 1:7 WHAT will they have if they do all according to the law?

_____

Joshua 1:8 What did you learn about the book of the law?

"This book of the law _____ _____

depart from your _____, but you shall

_____ on it _____

and _____, so that you may be

_____ to _____ according to _____

that is _____ in it."

Joshua 1:8 WHAT will happen if they mediate (study and think on) the law day and night and do all that is written in the law? WHAT will God do?

"You will make your way _____,

and then you will have _____."

Joshua 1:9 WHAT did God command them?

"Be _____ and

_____!

Do not _____ or be

_____."

Joshua 1:9 WHAT did we see about the Lord God?

"The LORD your God is _____ you wherever you

_____."

Look back at Joshua 1. HOW many times did God tell Joshua

to be strong and courageous? _____ times.

God tells Joshua to cross the Jordan to the land that God has promised to Abraham and all his descendants, the sons of Israel. The land is promised to them, but they have to go in and take the land from their enemies.

God tells Joshua; "No one will be able to stand before you all the days of your life; I will be with you; I will not fail you or forsake you." *Fail* means abandon, to let drop. *Forsake* means to loosen, depart, or to abandon. Joshua can take the land without fear, because God will never abandon, loosen His hold on, or leave Joshua.

God tells Joshua to be *strong* (to grip or fasten on to God). God says to be *courageous* (to be alert physically and mentally, to not fall apart). Joshua is not to tremble or be *dismayed* (to be broken down by fear, or confusion), because God is going to be with him ALL of the days of his life.

Isn't that AWESOME! Hold up your left arm, flex your muscle, and say: "Be strong." Now lift up your right arm, flex that muscle, and say: "and courageous" to remind you to hold on to God. Fasten on to Him instead of falling apart or breaking into fear! God is with you! God will not loosen His hold on you!

Did you notice how important the book of the law is? You read about the book of the law last week when we looked at Deuteronomy 17 and 31. The law is *so* important, and this week we learned that the Israelites are not to turn from the law, to the right or the left, so they may have success wherever they go. The law is not to depart from their mouth, rather they are to meditate on it (study and think about it) day and night and do all that is written in it so they will be prosperous and have success. WHAT is the key to having success? The law—God's Word! God's Word is the truth. It is what teaches us who God is, how to know and fear God, and how we are to live. Look at this verse:

2 Timothy 3:16-17

16 All Scripture is inspired by God and profitable for teaching, for reproof, for corrections, for training in righteousness;

17 so that the man of God may be adequate, equipped for every good work.

Second Timothy 3:16 tells us all Scripture (the Bible) is inspired by God. *Inspired* means "God-breathed." The Bible doesn't just *contain* God's words; it *is* the very words of God! We aren't just to know God's Word and meditate (to study and think on it). We are to do all that is written in it. We are to fear God—to honor and respect Him as God. We are to do what God says!

Look back at 2 Timothy 3:16 and circle the four things that the Scripture is PROFITABLE for. Then list the four things on the lines below.

_____

_____

_____

_____

God's Word teaches us so we can know the truth. It reproves us so we can know when we are doing something wrong. It corrects us so we can change what we have done wrong and know how to get it right. It trains us in righteousness so we can have a right relationship with God.

Have you been memorizing your memory verses (God's Word) to help you when you are afraid? _____

Are you learning and doing what God says? _____

Name one thing you are doing from God's Word.

_____

WHAT did you learn about God that will help you be strong and courageous when you are afraid?

_____

Do your hand signal to remind you to be strong and courageous when you feel afraid. Fantastic! HOW should you begin your BIG climb, Team Truth? With God's Truth. Solve your memory verse below to help you know what God says you should do when you face a big challenge and feel afraid.

Look at the first line of letters on Mount Triumph. Starting on the far right, write each letter for each word from right to left starting with the first blank on the first line on page 148. When you finish the first line, do the same thing for each word on the next four lines of letters to unscramble your memory verse.

MOUNT TRIUMPH

TON I EVAH

UOY DEDNAMMOC

SUOEGARUOC DNA GNORTS EB

DEYAMSID EB RO ELBMERT TON OD

HTIW SI DOG RUOY DROL EHT ROF

9:1 AUHSOJ OG UOY REVEREHW UOY

"_____ __ _____

_____ _____?

___ _____ _____ _____!

_____ ____ _____ __ ____ ____

____ _____,

____ ___ _____ ____ ___ ____

___ ____ ___

_____ _____ ____."

_____ __:__

You did it! Now write out your memory verse on a piece of paper and practice saying it out loud three times in a row, three times today!

Will you trust that God is with you no matter how hard or scary it is? Will you be strong and courageous like Joshua? Trust God. He will give you a brave heart just like He did for Joshua. God will not fail or forsake you!

Remember there is NO ONE stronger than God! Do your "be strong and courageous" hand signal one more time!

PUT ON YOUR ARMOR

You did a great job learning to climb Mount Triumph! Today we have another challenging adventure. We are going white water rafting. Are you ready to head to the river?

Great! Grab your paddles, helmets, and life jackets. Before we get on the river, we need to make sure everyone is equipped for this fun adventure.

You have discovered how David, King Jehoshaphat, and Joshua all had enemies. Do you have an enemy? Let's find out if you have an enemy, WHO it is, and WHAT you should do when your enemy comes against you. Don't forget to pray! Ask God to lead and guide you as you get ready to ride the rapids.

Read 1 Peter 5:8. Mark this key word:

adversary (devil) (draw a red pitchfork like this:)

> Be of sober *spirit*, be on the alert. Your adversary, the devil, prowls around like a roaring lion, seeking someone to devour (1 Peter 5:8).

1 Peter 5:8 WHO is your adversary?

_____

An adversary is an opponent, someone who is against you, an enemy.

1 Peter 5:8 WHAT does the devil want to do to you?

_____

To devour is to eat up greedily. The devil is like a hungry roaring lion who wants to eat you up. He is your adversary (your enemy). The devil wants to destroy you!

1 Peter 5:8 WHAT are you to be?

Be _____ the _____.

To be on the alert means to be watchful for danger. You need to know WHO your enemy is and WHAT he is like so he can't devour (destroy) you.

Read John 8:44 printed out below and mark the key words listed.

devil (draw a red pitchfork like this:)

you (This "you" is someone who is an enemy of God.) (color it red)

Don't forget to mark the pronouns for the devil!

> You are of *your* father the devil, and you want to do the desires of your father. He was a murderer from the beginning, and does not stand in truth because there is no truth in him. Whenever he speaks a lie, he speaks from his own *nature*, for he is a liar, and the father of lies (John 8:44).

Look at John 8:44. WHAT is the devil like? Complete the list of WHAT the devil is like in the box below.

WHAT I LEARNED ABOUT THE DEVIL

He was a _____ from the beginning.

He does not _____ in truth.

There is no _____ in him.

He is a _____ and the father of _____.

Did you notice your enemy, the devil, is a liar? Do you do things the devil does? Do you lie, or tell the truth? WHAT do you do?

_____

That's why we are not to lie because lying is what the devil does. The devil is the father of lies—there is no truth in him.

WHO is the truth? G __ d and J __ __ __ s!

Remember the devil is evil. He was a murderer from the beginning who wants to destroy you.

WHO is greater, the devil or God? _____

God is! God is good and only does what is good. God isn't afraid of ANYONE or ANYTHING!

Let's find out WHAT you should do when your enemy, the devil (who is also called Satan), comes after you. Turn to page 235. Read Ephesians 6:10-18 and mark the key phrases and the key words listed below.

be strong (strength) (box it in green)

God (Lord) (draw a purple triangle and color it yellow)

Put on the full armor of God (take up) (circle it in blue)

Stand firm (box it in orange)

devil (the evil one, rulers, power, and forces) (draw a red pitchfork like this:)

be on the alert (underline it in red)

pray (prayer) (draw a purple ⌣ and color it pink)

Ask the 5 Ws and an H questions.

Ephesians 6:10 WHAT is the first thing we are to do?

_____

Ephesians 6:11 WHAT are we to put on?

_____

Did you notice WHOSE armor it is? WHOSE is it?

_____

Ephesians 6:11 WHAT will the armor enable us to do?

_____

_____

Did you know the devil schemes against us? *Schemes* means a secret plan to come against another person. The devil makes plans to come against us. The devil wants to defeat us.

Ephesians 6:12 As Christians, WHO is our struggle against?

Is it against flesh and blood? _____

WHO is our struggle against?

"Against the _____, against the

_____, against the _____ _____

of this _____, against the

_____ _____ of _____

in the _____ _____."

Our battle isn't against people and the world. God tells us our struggle is against Satan and his spiritual forces of wickedness in the heavenly places. People and hard situations on earth may cause us trouble and make us afraid, but our real enemy is Satan (the devil) who causes our struggles on earth. Fear and lies are from Satan. Truth is from God.

Ephesians 6:13 HOW are we to stand? _____

Ephesians 6:14 WHAT are you to gird your loins with?

_____

Ephesians 6:14 WHAT kind of breastplate are you to put on?

_____

Ephesians 6:15 WHAT are you to put on your feet?

_____

_____

Ephesians 6:16 WHAT kind of shield do you put on?

_____

Ephesians 6:16 WHAT are you able to do with the shield of faith?

"You will be able to _____ all

the _____ _____ of the

_____ _____."

Ephesians 6:17 WHAT kind of helmet do you put on?

_____

Ephesians 6:18 WHAT are we to do at all times?

_____

When we come against the enemy we are not to surrender; we

are to stand firm. We need to put on the armor of God; we are to be strong in the Lord and the strength of His might. Remember your hand signal for being strong and courageous? Do it!

Let's practice putting on our spiritual armor by learning what each piece of the armor of God represents and how you are to use it. Look at the soldier below. As you read about each piece of armor, write its name on the line next to that piece of armor, and color it.

The first thing you are to do is to *Gird your loins with truth.* On the line next to the belt, write out **"the belt of truth."** Color the belt. Soldiers used a belt around their waist to hold their garments together and to keep each piece of armor in place. The belt is a symbol of strength. How can we put on the belt of truth? By daily studying God's Word, the truth, just like you are doing right now. We learned that our enemy is a liar and that there is no truth in him. We need to know the truth so that when our enemy comes against us, we can recognize the enemy's lie and fight him with God's Word—which is pure truth.

When you are afraid, fight your fear by tightening the belt of truth and say God's Word out loud. WHAT did Jesus tell the disciples? "Take Courage, It is I, do not be afraid." Remember Jesus is with you!

Put on the breastplate of righteousness. Write out **"the breastplate of righteousness"** on the line next to the breastplate and color it. Soldiers wore the breastplate to protect their vital organs, like the heart, lungs, stomach, and kidneys, so the enemy's arrows could not get through and kill them. Protect yourself with the breastplate of righteousness. God always does the right thing, and that's what He wants us to do. We can do the right thing by staying away from sin and doing what God says in His Word. Then the enemy can't defeat us! Do your actions show that you belong to Jesus? Do you do what God says is right? Do you confess your sins when you don't do the right thing? Remember, God always does what is right. Ask God to help you do what is right!

Shod your feet with the preparation of the gospel of peace. Write out **"sandals of the gospel of peace"** on the line next to the sandals and color them. In Roman times the sandals weren't slick on the bottom, they had "grippers" so they could stand firm—not be shaken.

When you know that you belong to God, then there is peace in your heart. You are on God's side and He's on yours. The devil can't win against God!

When you are afraid, put on the shoes of peace you have in

Jesus, and remember WHO you belong to, so you will be able to stand firm and not be shaken by the enemy's lies, threats, and your fear. Have you shared the good news about Jesus with one of your friends? Truth becomes more firmly placed in our hearts when we share it.

Take up the shield of faith. Write out **"shield of faith"** next to the shield and color it. The shield enabled the soldier to put out the flaming arrows directed at him. The shield was made of leather and soaked in water so when those fiery missiles came at them, they would sizzle out when they hit the shield.

Whenever the enemy throws a lie, doubt, or accusation at you, just hold up God's Word and say, "But God says…", and then give the devil a verse that counteracts it. That's the way Jesus won against the devil when He was tempted in the wilderness. The more you know God's Word, the stronger your shield will be. Soak your shield in the water of God's Word every day, just like you are doing right now, and the enemy won't be able to get to you. Do you trust God? Do you turn to Him when bad things happen, and you are afraid?

When you are afraid, hold up your shield and put that flaming arrow out. Tell the devil, "'You who fear the LORD, trust in the LORD; He is their help and their shield' (Psalm 115:11). God will protect and help me!"

Take the helmet of salvation. Write out **"helmet of salvation"** on the line next to the helmet and color it. Soldiers wore a helmet to protect their head from deadly blows. We need to protect our minds by remembering whom we belong to. Christ lives inside of Christians and He is stronger than the enemy. Greater is He who is in you than he, the devil (and his demons), who are in the world. Have you asked Jesus to be your Savior?

Put your helmet on! When you are afraid, protect your mind

from the enemy's lies. Remember it's the helmet of salvation. If you have given your life to Jesus, you are God's child! God loves you! You belong to Him!

Take the sword of the Spirit. Write out **"the sword of the Spirit"** on the line next to the sword and color it. The sword of the Spirit is God's Word. It's our only offensive weapon because it is all we need for victory. The only way we can fight the enemy is with God's Word. When you are afraid, pull that sword out of its sheath and use it! Remember God's Word. Say it out loud, "When I am afraid I will put my trust in You" (Psalm 56:3). God says in Joshua 1:9, "Be strong and courageous! Do not tremble or be dismayed. For the LORD your God is with you wherever you go." You can't see God, but He is with you. You are never alone. Tell God, "I will trust You. I will hold on tight to You. You are with me. You won't abandon me!" Do your "be strong and courageous" hand signal.

WHAT are you to do at all times? P __ __ __! Cry out to God, praise Him for who He is, thank Him for giving you His strength.

You did it! Practice putting your armor on so that you can win the battle every day of your life! Remember, you are to be strong in the Lord and in the strength of His might by putting on the full armor of God. All the armor centers around the Word of God. That's the only way to win the battle against fear and your enemy, Satan. Trust God. Fear Him, not man or Satan. Honor and respect God by knowing and obeying His Word! Just like David, King Jehoshaphat, and Joshua—God will fight for you!

Say your memory verse out loud! WHAT are you to do? WHO is with you? Way to go! Now you are equipped to ride the rapids.

DON'T LET YOUR HEART BE TROUBLED

Are you enjoying challenge week at Camp Braveheart? As we conquer each challenge, we learn more about how we can trust God and have a brave heart in scary and difficult circumstances.

Today we are going to discover a challenge the disciples faced when Jesus tells them the time has come for Him to go away. Let's find out WHAT Jesus says to His disciples. Pray and ask God to help you when you are afraid and when things are hard to understand and don't happen the way you thought or hoped they would turn out.

Turn to page 235. Read John 14:1-3, 27 and mark the key words listed below.

heart (draw a red heart on it)

troubled (fearful) (draw a black jagged circle around it)

believe (draw a purple book like this: and color the inside green)

Me (My, I, Myself—that's Jesus) (draw a purple cross and color it yellow)

peace (color it blue)

Ask the 5 Ws and an H questions.

John 14:1 WHAT did Jesus say to the disciples?

"Do not _____ your _____ be

_____."

WHY did Jesus tell the disciples, "Do not let your heart be troubled"? In John 13:33, Jesus had just told the disciples He is going away, and they can't come with Him. Jesus is comforting the disciples. He knows the disciples are upset and troubled over Jesus leaving.

Look back at John 14:1. WHAT did Jesus tell them after He tells them not to let their hearts be troubled?

"_____ in _____,

_____ also in _____."

Jesus tells the disciples not to be upset or worried but to believe in God and in Him. Trusting Jesus and God comforts our troubled heart.

John 14:2 WHERE is Jesus going?

_____

John 14:2 WHAT does Jesus say about His Father's house?

_____

_____

John 14:2 WHY is Jesus going there?

_____

_____

John 14:3 WHAT will Jesus do after He prepares a place for us?

_____

_____

Jesus is going back to His Father's house in heaven to prepare a place for us! Jesus is going away by dying on a cross to save us from our sins, but He will come again to take us to live with Him!

Look at John 14:27. WHAT is Jesus going to give them?

_____

WHAT kind of peace? Is it the peace that the world gives, or the peace that only Jesus can give?

_____

_____

John 14:27 WHAT does Jesus say about their hearts?

_____

_____

Read Isaiah 9:6 printed out below. Isaiah is giving us a prophecy about Jesus. A prophecy is sort of like a secret. It is when God reveals to us what is going to happen in the future.

> For a child will be born to us, a son will be given to us;
> And the government will rest on His shoulders;
> And His name will be called Wonderful Counselor,
> Mighty God, Eternal Father, Prince of Peace (Isaiah 9:6).

WHO is Jesus?

_____

_____

Isn't that awesome to see WHO Jesus is! WHAT is Jesus Prince

of? _____

We don't have to be troubled or afraid when things happen that we don't understand. We can choose to trust Jesus. Jesus is the Wonderful Counselor, Mighty God, Eternal Father, and Prince of Peace. When we believe, we put our trust in Jesus—the Prince of Peace. It doesn't matter what is happening to us; Jesus is our peace when we choose to trust Him.

Let's see WHAT Jesus says in John 16:33—

> These things I have spoken to you, so that in Me you
> may have peace. In the world you have tribulation, but
> take courage; I have overcome the world.

John 16:33 WHY did Jesus tell us these things?

"So that in _____ you may have _____."

John 16:33 WHAT do we have in the world?

_____

John 16:33 WHAT does Jesus tell us to do?

_____ _____

WHY? WHAT has Jesus done?

Jesus has _____ the

_____.

In this world we will have tribulations, trouble, and hard times. There will be tornados, wars, pandemics, sickness, diseases, and death. People will go hungry and be hurt. There will be things that upset and worry us BUT Jesus tells us to take courage. We can be comforted, courageous, and full of cheer because Jesus has overcome the world!

We have peace in Jesus because Jesus defeated sin and Satan, the ruler of this world, when He died on the cross to pay for our sins, was buried, and was resurrected. God raised Jesus from the dead on the third day! Jesus is the Overcomer! And when you are saved by faith in Jesus, you become an overcomer too! God tells us in 1 John 5:5 that we overcome the world by our faith in Jesus—by believing what God says about Him!

In this world we will have trouble, but Jesus is our Peace, Jesus has overcome the world, and one day very soon Jesus will come back and take us to live with God and Him forever!

Now say your memory verse out loud three times in a row, three times today!

Remember when you have a troubled heart you can have peace by trusting Jesus. Trusting God and Jesus is the ONLY way to overcome our troubled hearts. Remember your hand signal for faith conquers fear. Do it!

DAY FOUR

FiX YOUR MiND ON GOD

Are you ready for your next challenge? Today we are going to climb up to the top of the hill and zipline down across the lake. It's going to be a wild wet ride. Don't forget to hold on tight. Race you to the other side. Yahooooo!

You did great as you bounced across the lake. What a brave heart! Yesterday we learned when our hearts are troubled, we need to trust Jesus—the Prince of Peace. Today, let's find out WHAT God has given us to help us do that.

Read 2 Timothy 1:7. Mark the key words listed.

timidity (draw a black jagged circle around it)

power (draw a red stick of dynamite like this: ⬭)

love (draw a red heart and color it red)

discipline (box it in blue)

For God has not given us a spirit of timidity, but of power and love and discipline (2 Timothy 1:7).

2 Timothy 1:7 WHAT hasn't God given us?

A _____ of _____.

How amazing is that? God has not given us a spirit of fear. We are not to fear man or what He can do to us. Think about what you learned in Psalm 56:3 (one of your memory verses). HOW can you keep from being afraid? Can you fill in the blanks for Psalm 56:3 without looking?

Psalm 56:3 "When I am afraid, I will _____ my

_____ in You."

God has not given us a spirit of fear. Do you remember your hand signal for faith over fear? Do it.

Look back at 2 Timothy 1:7. WHAT has God given us?

A spirit of _____ and _____ and

_____.

Do you remember what you learned about receiving God's power in Acts 1:8? Turn to page 106. Read Acts 1:8.

Acts 1:8 HOW do you receive power?

"When the _____ _____ has

_____ upon you."

When you become a child of God, God's Spirit comes to live in you! You have God's POWER!

Look back at 2 Timothy 1:7 on page 166. WHAT do we have besides power? L __ __ __.

HOW do we have love? Turn to page 231. Read John 3:16.

John 3:16 HOW does God show His love for us?

"God so _____ the world, that He

gave His only begotten _____, that whoever

_____ in Him shall not perish, but

have _____ _____."

Do you remember how to make a heart with your hands and fingers? Take your fingers on both hands and put them together to make a heart and place it over your heart to remind you how much God loves you!

Read 1 John 4:11 printed out below. Mark the key word listed.

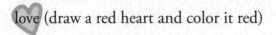 love (draw a red heart and color it red)

Beloved, if God so loved us, we also ought to love one another (1 John 4:11).

1 John 4:11 WHAT are we to do since God loves us?

_____

Read 1 John 4:18 printed out below. Mark the key words listed.

fear (draw a black jagged circle around it)

love (draw a red heart and color it red)

There is no fear in love; but perfect love casts out fear, because fear involves punishment, and the one who fears is not perfected in love (1 John 4:18).

1 John 4:18 WHAT do we see about love in this verse?

Perfect love casts out _____.

Because of God's great love and sacrifice for us, we don't have to be afraid. Perfect love casts out fear. And because of God's great love for us, we are to love others!

Look back at 2 Timothy 1:7 WHAT is the last thing God has given us?

D __ __ __ __ __ __ __ __ __

That means to have a sound mind, to have self-control. It means we have our mind under control. HOW can we be disciplined? HOW do we have a steadfast mind? Read Isaiah 26:3—

> The steadfast of mind You will keep in perfect peace, because he trusts in You.

Look at Isaiah 26:3. HOW do you have a steadfast mind?

_____

Isaiah 26:3 HOW does God keep a person with a steadfast mind?

In _____ _____

You did great! God has not given you a spirit of fear. You have God's power, love, and a disciplined, steadfast mind. When you are afraid, remember God loves you! You can discipline your mind, train it, and keep it under control by putting your trust in God and His power. When you fix your mind on God and put your trust in Him, He will keep you in perfect peace! Isn't that AWESOME?

Don't forget to practice your memory verse!

GUARD YOUR HEART AND MIND

How do you like challenge week at Camp Braveheart? You have hiked through the forest, climbed Mount Triumph, braved the whitewater rapids, and zip lined down the hill and across the lake. Today we are going to challenge Team Hope in a game of tug-of-war.

Tug-of-war is fun game of strength, weakness, and strategy where two teams pull on opposite ends of a rope. The goal is to for each team to pull the rope with the opposite team to their side of the tug line. Whoever pulls the opposite team across the line wins.

Are you ready to strategize and create a plan to beat Team Hope? Before you do, let's find out how God tells us to win the "tug-of-war" in our minds when we are anxious and afraid. Talk to God and ask God to show you how to handle anxious feelings.

Let's look at the New Testament book of Philippians. Did you know the apostle Paul wrote this letter to the believers (those who belong to Jesus) when he was suffering and in prison? An *apostle* means Paul was a messenger of the good news about Jesus Christ.

Paul is serving God by telling other people the good news about Jesus.

WHY would God allow Paul, His chosen messenger, to be in prison? Because God knew there was a Roman jailer with a family who needed to know Jesus. Let's find out how Paul handles some hard and difficult circumstances to serve God.

Turn to page 236. Read Philippians 4:6-13. Mark the key words listed below.

prayer (draw a purple ⌣ and color it pink)

heart (draw a red heart)

mind (circle it in blue)

Christ Jesus (Lord, Him) (draw a purple cross and color it yellow)

peace (color it blue)

circumstance (color it orange)

Mark Paul's instructions by boxing the instruction in green. An instruction is a specific "do this" or "don't do that" command. WHAT does Paul say to do or not to do?

Ask the 5 Ws and an H questions.

Philippians 4:6 WHAT are we not to do?

"Be _____ for nothing."

To be anxious means to be troubled with cares. We get anxious when we can't get our worries off our mind.

Philippians 4:6 WHAT are we to do when we are anxious?

"In everything by _____ and supplication with

_____ let your requests
be made known to God."

When we are anxious and afraid, we need tools to help us stop.
HOW do we stop worrying? PRAY! We need to talk to God. We
need to remember WHO God is. Praying takes our minds off our
worry or fear and puts our mind on God. We need to pray with
supplication (to seek, ask, and plead with God humbly for help)
and with thanksgiving (giving thanks and worship). Our best
defense against worries is to talk to God and thank Him for WHO
He is and HOW He provides.

Name something that makes you anxious and afraid, that you
need God to help you with.

_____

WHAT are you thankful for?

_____

Philippians 4:7 If we pray, thank God, and give Him our
requests, WHAT will we have?

"The _____ of God, which

_____ all comprehension."

When we pray, give our worries to God, and focus on what we

have to be thankful for, God will give us His peace that goes way beyond what we can understand. Isn't that AWESOME?

Philippians 4:7 WHAT will God's peace do?

"_____ your _____ and your

_____ in Christ Jesus."

God's peace will guard (protect, keep) our hearts and our minds in Christ Jesus. Worry hurts our minds and our bodies. Being thankful gives us God's peace that is beyond anything we can imagine, protecting our hearts and our minds.

Philippians 4:8 WHAT are we to dwell (let our minds think) on?

"Whatever is _____, whatever is

_____, whatever is

_____, whatever is _____, what-

ever is _____, whatever is of _____ repute, if there is any excellence and if anything worthy of

_____, dwell on these things."

Read 2 Corinthians 10:5—

We are destroying speculations and every lofty thing raised up against the knowledge of God, and *we are* taking every thought captive to the obedience of Christ.

Look at 2 Corinthians 10:5. WHAT are you to do with your thoughts?

Take every thought _____ through the obedience of Christ.

What we see, hear, and think affects our feelings. Our thoughts are so important; we need to be careful what we think. When you have an anxious thought, grab it, and hold it captive—does it measure up to what you just learned in Philippians 4:8? Is it good, true, right, does it honor God, is it excellent and worthy of praise? If it isn't, then STOP thinking it. Replace it with thoughts that are good. Think about WHO God is, how much He loves you, and WHAT you are thankful for. Being thankful and joyful gives you God's peace and takes away your stress and worry. A thankful heart will remind you of God's goodness!

Look back at Philippians 4:9 WHAT are we to do?

_____ these things.

Practice means to do it over and over again. Practice thinking on what is good, true, right, honoring to God, and is excellent and worthy of praise. Do this over and over when you feel afraid or anxious. Don't let fear and anxious thoughts play "tug-of-war" and pull you away from trusting God.

Philippians 4:11 WHAT did Paul say?

"I have learned to be _____ in whatever

_____ I am."

Paul chooses to be *content* (peaceful, satisfied, a calm acceptance) no matter the circumstances: whether he is in prison, out of prison, whether he has a lot or a little, whether he is hungry or filled, and whether things are good or bad.

Look at Philippians 4:13. WHAT does Paul say? HOW is Paul able to be content?

"I can do _____ things through Him (Jesus) who

_____ me."

Paul gets His strength through Jesus! Jesus will give us His strength to help us in whatever situation we are in.
Read 1 Peter 5:7—

Casting all your anxiety on Him, because He cares for you.

1 Peter 5:7 WHAT are you to do?

_____ all your _____ on Him.

To cast means to throw, to roll it over on to God's shoulders. It's like taking off your backpack and putting it on God. Take all your worries, your fears, and your cares and roll them on to God's shoulders.

WHY? Because He _____ for you.

Isn't that AMAZING? God takes all your cares and puts them on Himself because He cares for you!

You did it! You know how to win the "tug-of-war" of feeling anxious and afraid. WHAT are you going to do the next time you have an anxious or fearful thought?

_____

_____

Say your memory verse out loud to a grown-up. Thinking about all you have learned this week, **WHAT should you do when you are afraid?**

1. **Be strong and courageous**—God is with me. God will not abandon me or let me go. Do your hand signal for strong and courageous.

2. **Put my armor on**—Satan is a liar and a murderer who wants me to be afraid. I will be strong in the Lord and the strength of His might. I will put my armor on.

3. **Remember Jesus is my peace**—When my heart is troubled, I will trust Jesus, the Prince of Peace. In this world I will have hard times, but I can take courage (be comforted) because Jesus is the Overcomer. When I put my faith in Jesus, I am an overcomer too!

4. **Remember I have God's power, love, and discipline**—God has not given me a spirit of fear but a spirit of power, love, and discipline. The Holy Spirt gives me His power. I have God's perfect love. I can discipline my mind. I can control what I think.

5. **Cast my anxiety on God**—I will roll my worries and fears on to God. I will pray and ask God to help me. I will give thanks because God's got this. I will take every

thought captive. I will think (keep my mind on) and practice whatever is true, right, honoring to God, good, excellent, and worthy of praise. I will BE CONTENT in all my circumstances because God is sovereign. I can do all things through Jesus who gives me strength.

WHO iS YOUR HOPE?

Are you ready for your last week at Camp Braveheart? Last week, we saw God prepare Joshua to go in and take the promised land from his enemies. We are to be strong and courageous like Joshua. God is with us. He will not abandon or leave us! Do your hand signal. In this world we will have trouble, because Satan is trying to defeat us. But we can be strong in the Lord by putting on the full armor of God.

We also saw that Jesus will give us His peace when our hearts are troubled. Jesus overcame the world and defeated Satan when He died on the cross and was resurrected three days later. When we believe in Jesus, we are overcomers too! God has not given us a spirit of fear, but of power, love, and discipline. We can cast all our cares on God because God cares for us! Isn't that AWESOME and AMAZING?

This week we are going to discover WHY God allows hard and difficult things in our lives. WHAT is God's plan for us? WHO is our hope? And HOW we can rest in God.

YOU ARE NEVER ALONE

Come on over, Team Truth! Today we are heading into the woods for a scavenger hunt.

The winner is the first team to solve their clues, gather the things on their list, and make it back to camp. After all the teams make it back, we will start a fire and make s'mores under the stars. Is everyone ready? Great! Talk to God. Now we're ready to go! Read Genesis 37:2-4 printed out below. Mark the key words listed.

Joseph (color it blue)

love (draw and color a red heart)

hate (draw and color a black heart with a zigzag line through it)

Don't forget to mark your pronouns!

Genesis 37:2-4

2 These are *the records of* the generations of Jacob. Joseph, when seventeen years of age, was pasturing the flock with his brothers while he was *still* a youth, along with the sons of Bilhah and the sons of Zilpah, his father's wives. And Joseph brought back a bad report about them to their father.

3 Now Israel loved Joseph more than all his sons, because he was the son of his old age; and he made him a varicolored tunic.

4 His brothers saw that their father loved him more than all his brothers; and *so* they hated him and could not speak to him on friendly terms.

Ask the 5 Ws and an H questions.

Genesis 37:2 HOW old was Joseph? _____ years old.

Genesis 37:3 HOW did Joseph's father (Israel) feel about Joseph?

_____

Did you know that Israel and Jacob are the same person? God changed Joseph's father's name from Jacob to Israel in Genesis 35:9-10.

Genesis 37:4 HOW did the brothers feel about Joseph?

_____

WHY?

_____

_____

Look at Genesis 37:18—

> When they saw him from a distance and before he came close to them, they plotted against him to put him to death.

Genesis 37:18 WHAT did the brothers plot to do to Joseph?

_____

WOW! Joseph's brothers hated Joseph so much that they plotted to kill him. They stripped him of his special varicolored tunic, a gift from their father, and threw him into a pit. Judah (one of the brothers) later convinces the other brothers to sell Joseph instead of killing him. Joseph is sold as a slave and taken far from his home to

Egypt and sold to Potiphar, an Egyptian officer of Pharaoh who is the captain of the bodyguard. WHAT happens next? Turn to page 236. Read Genesis 39:1-6 and mark the key words listed below.

Joseph (color it blue)

The LORD was with Joseph (the LORD was with him) (circle it in purple)

favor (color it yellow)

blessed (blessing) (draw a blue cloud around it and color it pink)

Don't forget to mark your pronouns!

Look at Genesis 39:2. Is Joseph alone? WHO was with Joseph?

_____ _____

Genesis 39:3-4 WHAT did the Lord cause to happen?

_____

_____

Joseph is 17-year-old boy, kidnapped from his home by his brothers. Joseph has gone from being popular with Papa to being thrown in a pit and sold as a slave to Potiphar. But look at how much God loves Joseph. God was with Joseph. God caused all of Joseph's work to prosper. Even though Joseph is a slave, he becomes a successful man.

In Genesis 39:7-20, while Joseph is Potiphar's slave, he is accused by Potiphar's wife of something he didn't do and is thrown into prison. WHAT happens next?

Genesis 39:21-23

21 The LORD was with Joseph and extended kindness to him, and gave him favor in the sight of the chief jailer.

22 The chief jailer committed to Joseph's charge all the prisoners who were in the jail; so that whatever was done there, he was responsible for it.

23 …the LORD was with him; and whatever he did, the LORD made to prosper.

Look at Genesis 39:21. WHAT did God do while Joseph was in prison?

"The _____ was _____ Joseph and

extended _____ to him and gave him

_____ in the sight of the chief jailer."

Genesis 39:22 WHAT did the chief jailer commit to Joseph's charge?

All the _____ who were in the jail.

Is Joseph alone? No! God is with Joseph extending kindness to him. God gives Joseph favor in the sight of the chief jailer. Even in jail, the Lord causes everything Joseph does to prosper. Joseph is put in charge of all the prisoners. God is using Joseph's hard circumstance for Joseph's good!

HOW would you feel if you were kidnapped from home by your own brothers, sold as a slave, and then put in jail for something you didn't do? Would you feel scared, lonely, and rejected, or angry and determined to get even? Would you feel that God didn't love you and had abandoned you? Write out HOW you would feel.

_____

_____

_____

Most people would be angry or bitter at God, but what did Joseph do? Joseph trusted God. He never grew angry or bitter. Joseph had courage. Even when he didn't understand, Joseph trusted God. Tomorrow we will find out WHAT happens next to Joseph.

Way to go! You made it to the campfire first. Look up at the stars in the picture on page 186 to discover your memory verse this week. Each star has a word from your verse that has been written backwards. Start with the first star and write each letter in the star from right to left. Then, place the correct word on the blanks underneath the picture.

"In _____ I _____ both

_____ _____ and _____,

_____ _____ _____, O

_____, _____ _____ to _____

_____ _____." Psalm 4:8

Great work! Now write this verse out on a piece of paper and practice saying it out loud three times in a row, three times today! Isn't God wonderful?

WHY DOES GOD ALLOW BAD THINGS TO HAPPEN?

You did great on your scavenger hunt yesterday! Today, we are heading back into the woods to develop our teamwork skills as we work our way through an obstacle course. This will help us as we look more closely at the unexpected obstacles in Joseph's life.

Today, as we scale walls, crawl through tunnels, walk across beams, and climb ropes on our obstacle course, let's find out HOW God used all the hard situations in Joseph's life for good. Pray and ask God to teach and encourage you.

While Joseph is in prison, two of Pharaoh's officials, the chief cupbearer and the chief baker, are thrown in jail with him. Both the chief cupbearer and the chief baker have a dream. Read Genesis 40:8 to find out what happens.

Then they said to him, "We have had a dream and there is no one to interpret it." Then Joseph said to them, "Do not interpretations belong to God? Tell *it* to me, please" (Genesis 40:8).

WHO did Joseph say the interpretations belonged to?

_____

Joseph knows God is the one who interprets dreams. God gives Joseph the interpretations of both dreams. Joseph tells the chief cupbearer that his dream means he will be restored to his position, but the chief baker's dream means he will be hanged, and the birds will eat his flesh.

When the chief cupbearer is released from prison, Joseph asks him to remember him. The chief cupbearer is restored but instead of remembering Joseph, he forgets about him.

After two years, Pharoah has a dream that no one can interpret. The cupbearer remembers Joseph and tells Pharoah about Joseph interpreting his dream. WHAT happens next? Open your Bible and read Genesis 41:25-28.

Genesis 41:25-28 WHO does Joseph point Pharaoh to?

_____

Even though Joseph has been mistreated by his brothers, sold as slave to Potiphar in Egypt, falsely accused for something he didn't do, and thrown in prison for two long years, WHOM does Joseph tell Pharaoh the interpretations belong to? WHO does Joseph point Pharaoh to as being in control? God!

Now read Genesis 41:39-46 in your Bible.

Genesis 41:41 WHO does God put in command over all the land of Egypt, second only to Pharaoh? _____

Genesis 41:46 HOW old was Joseph when he stood before Pharaoh? _____ years old.

Joseph was 17 years old when he was kidnapped and sold as slave. He is now 30 years old. WHY would God allow Joseph to be a slave and prisoner for 13 years? God had a plan. God put Joseph in the right place, in the right position, at the right time to rescue them from a famine. When the famine comes, Jacob sends his sons (Joseph's brothers) to Egypt to buy grain so they won't starve.

WHAT will Joseph do when he is reunited with his brothers? Remember, his brothers hated him so much they had sold him as a slave to Egypt. Turn in your Bible to Genesis 45:4-8 and read what it says.

Look at Genesis 45:5. WHAT does Joseph say to his brothers when he reveals himself to them?

"Do not be _____ or _____ with yourselves, because you _____ me here, for _____ sent me before you to _____ _____."

Genesis 45:7-8 WHO sent Joseph to Egypt? _____

Isn't that awesome? Joseph knows even though it was his brothers who sold him, it is God who is in control of all his circumstances.

Genesis 45:7 WHY did God send Joseph to Egypt?

"To _____ for you a

_____ in the earth, and to _____

you _____ by a great _____."

Now read Genesis 50:18-21 in your Bible.

Genesis 50:19 WHAT did Joseph say to his brothers?

"Do not _____ _____, for am I in

_____ _____?"

Genesis 50:20 WHAT were the brother's intentions?

_____

Genesis 50:20 WHAT were God's intentions?

_____

Genesis 50:21 HOW did Joseph treat the brothers who had mistreated him?

He p __ __ __ __ __ d for them,

_____them and spoke

_____ to them.

WOW! Can you believe it? Even though Joseph was hated and mistreated by his brothers, he tells them not to be afraid. Joseph tells his brothers he will provide for them and their children. He comforted them and spoke kindly to them. Joseph forgave his brothers.

HOW was Joseph able to forgive the brothers who hurt him? Joseph knew God is the sovereign ruler of the universe. He knew that God was the giver of the interpretations of the dreams, and he knew that God was the one who sent him to Egypt. He knew that even though his brothers wanted evil for him, God used his circumstances for good—to provide a great deliverance and to keep them alive during a famine. Joseph was able to bow his knee and surrender his will for God's. Isn't that AMAZING? Stop and think. If you are in a hard circumstance, WHAT might God be preparing you for? Can you think of a way God might use your circumstance to help you or someone else?

_____

Joseph was never alone. God was with him, extending His kindness and causing those in charge of Joseph to show him favor. God used 13 years of hard circumstances to shape and mold Joseph into a leader so He could use him to save a nation.

Open your Bible and read Romans 8:28-39. Answer the 5 Ws and an H questions below.

Romans 8:28 WHAT does God cause?

"God causes _____ _____ to

_____ _____ for good."

Romans 8:28 WHO does God do this for?

"To those who _____ _____ and

are _____ according to His

_____."

God doesn't say all things are good. God says if we love Him and are His children, then He causes ALL things—the good, the bad, the scary, and the ugly—to work together for our good and for His purpose, just like He did for Joseph. God took the bad and the ugly in Joseph's life and used it to save an entire nation.

WHAT might God do for you someday because you trust Him and do what He says even when its hard?

_____

Look at Romans 8:31. WHO is for us? _____

Romans 8:32 WHO didn't God spare to save us?

_____ _____ _____

Romans 8:32 WHAT will God and Jesus do for us?

Freely _____ us _____ _____.

Romans 8:34 WHO is at the right hand of God interceding for us?

_____ _____

Intercede means to pray in our favor. Did you know Jesus is in heaven praying for you?

Look at Romans 8:35. Can anything separate us from the love

of Christ? _____

Sometimes God doesn't deliver us in our hard situations but uses the hard situation to make us holy. To be *holy* means to be set apart to be used by God.

Look at Romans 8:37. WHAT are we able to do through Him who loves us?

In all these things we _____

_____.

Romans 8:38-39 List the things that can't separate us from the love of God in Christ Jesus our Lord.

"For I am convinced that neither _____,

nor _____, nor _____, nor

_____, nor

things _____ nor things to _____,

nor _____, nor _____, nor

_____, nor any other _____

thing, will be able to _____ us from the love of God which is in Christ Jesus our Lord."

You can trust God when you are afraid or when bad things

happen to you because God is in control. God is for us! There is absolutely NOTHING that can separate you from the love of God! God and Jesus love you! Jesus is in heaven praying for you!

Read 1 Thessalonians 5:18—

> In everything give thanks; for this is God's will for you
> in Christ Jesus.

WHAT is God's will for you?

_____

Will you do that? Will you give thanks to God even in the hard circumstances and when you are afraid? Remember, giving thanks puts your focus (your attention) on God and not your circumstances. Being thankful puts your hope and your trust in God. It will remind you of God's goodness and give you joy. When you practice being thankful, the God of all peace will give you His peace in your heart.

Write out a note of thanksgiving to God on the lines below. WHAT are you thankful for? Thank God for taking ALL things—the good, the bad, the things that make you afraid and that scare you, the things that make you anxious—and for working them together for you for good.

_____

_____

_____

Think about how you saw God work in Joseph's life. God was with Joseph in every situation: with his brothers' hatred, as a slave, when he was falsely accused, and when he was forgotten in prison. God was there extending His kindness to him. God took care of

Joseph and He will take care of you too! God is Sovereign. Because God rules over everything, we can bow our knees in surrender and give thanks to God in ALL things! Nothing in this world can separate us from the love of God in Jesus Christ. God will take all the scary, hard things and use them for our good and His purpose! Trust Him.

Don't forget to practice your memory verse! WHAT will God do?

WHO IS YOUR TRUST IN?

All right, Team Truth! Are you ready for a new challenge on the obstacle course with Team Hope? Great! We need to learn how to trust and encourage our teammates when the going gets hard so we can finish the course. But before we get started, let's find out what we are like when we put our trust in *man*, and what we are like when we trust God. Don't forget to pray and ask God to show you!

Read Jeremiah 17:5-8 printed out on page 196. Mark the key words listed.

cursed (draw a box in orange and color it brown)

trust (trusts) (draw a blue T over it)

blessed (draw a blue cloud around it and color it pink)

fear (anxious) (draw a black jagged circle around it)

Jeremiah 17:5-8

5 Thus says the LORD,
   "Cursed is the man who trusts in mankind
   And makes flesh his strength,
   And whose heart turns away from the LORD.

6 "For he will be like a bush in the desert
   And will not see when prosperity comes,
   But will live in stony wastes in the wilderness,
   A land of salt without inhabitant.

7 "Blessed is the man who trusts in the LORD
   And whose trust is the LORD.

8 "For he will be like a tree planted by the water,
   That extends its roots by a stream
   And will not fear when the heat comes;
   But its leaves will be green,
   And it will not be anxious in a year of drought
   Nor cease to yield fruit."

Ask the 5 Ws and an H questions to solve the crossword puzzle on page 198. WHAT is the difference in the person who trusts God and the person who puts his trusts in *man*?

Jeremiah 17:5 WHY is the man cursed? WHO does he place his trust in?

1. (Across) In _____

WHAT does he make his strength?

2. (Across) _____

Jeremiah 17:5 WHAT do we see about the cursed man's heart?

3. (Across) Whose heart _____

4. (Across) _____ from the LORD.

Jeremiah 17:6 WHAT will this cursed man be like?

5. (Down) A _____ in the

6. (Across) _____

He will live in stony wastes in the

7. (Down) _____

Jeremiah 17:7 WHY is this man blessed?

8. (Down) He _____ in the LORD.

Jeremiah 17:8 WHAT will the blessed man be like?

9. (Across) A _____ planted by the

10. (Down) _____ that extends its

11. (Across) _____ by a

12. (Down) _____.

He will not **13. (Down)** _____ when the
14. (Across) _____ comes; but its

15. (Down) _____ will be

16. (Down) _____,

It will not be **17. (Across)** _____ in a year of

18. (Down) _____

Nor cease to yield **19. (Across)** _____.

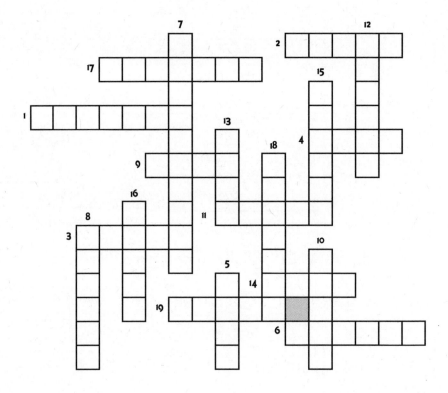

Draw a picture so that you can see the contrasts (the differences) in these two men in the boxes below. In the first box, draw the description of what the cursed man is like, and in the second box, draw a picture that describes the blessed man.

Cursed

Blessed

WHAT a difference in these two men! WHICH one do you want to be like, the one whose trust is in himself and is cursed, or the one whose trust is in the Lord and is blessed?

_____

Are you afraid when the heat (difficult time) comes? Or are you resting, because you know that the heat (difficult time) can't destroy you because you trust God and are rooted by a stream? Write out which one describes you.

_____

When we trust God, we will be like a tree that is planted by the water instead of a dry bush in the desert. We will not fear or be anxious when the heat and drought (hard times) come. We will yield fruit because our trust is in God!

Look at Isaiah 41:10—

> Do not fear, for I am with you;
> Do not anxiously look about you, for I am your God.
> I will strengthen you, surely I will help you,
> Surely I will uphold you with my righteous right hand.

Isaiah 41:10 WHY aren't you to fear?

_____

WHY aren't you to anxiously look about you?

_____

WHAT will God do?

God will _____ you.

God will _____ you.

God will _____ you with His

_____ _____

_____.

WHAT an AWESOME promise! Remember this verse the next time you feel anxious or afraid. Say it out loud! God is with you. God is your God. God will give you His strength. God will help you. Remember your hand signal for faith over fear? Your right hand (faith) covers your left, shaky hand (fear). Just as your right hand covers your left to stop you from shaking, God will hold you with His righteous right hand! If you trust God, you will be like a tree planted by a stream with green leaves bearing fruit—even when the hard times come! You will be blessed!

Don't Be Frightened or Misled

Good morning, Team Truth! Are you ready to play capture the flag one more time? Great! Grab your Map. We are ready to play. Talk to God and ask Him to teach you HOW you can have hope in scary and difficult times.

Turn to page 237. Read Matthew 24:3-8 and mark the following key words.

Jesus (draw a purple cross and color it yellow)

sign (draw a red sign like this:)

Your coming (This is Jesus's second coming) (draw a purple cloud around it and color it in three parts: the first part blue, the middle part yellow, and the last part blue) frightened (draw a black jagged circle around it)

wars (circle it in black)

nations (underline it in brown and color it green)

famines (box it in black and color it brown)

earthquakes (draw a brown jagged line like this:)

Don't forget to mark your pronouns for Jesus! Mark anything that tells you WHEN by drawing a green circle ◯ or a green clock like this: 🕐

Ask the 5 Ws and an H questions.

Matthew 24:3 WHAT do the disciples ask Jesus?

"_____ will these _____

_____, and what *will be* the _____

of Your _____, and of the _____ of the

_____?"

Matthew 24:4 WHAT are they not to let anyone do?

"See to it that no one _____ you."

Matthew 24:6 WHAT will they hear about?

_____

Matthew 24:6 WHAT does Jesus tell them not to do when they hear about these things?

You are not to be _____.

WHY? Because those _____ _____

take _____.

Matthew 24:7 WHAT does Jesus say the nations will do?

Nation will _____ _____ nation.

Matthew 24:7 WHAT will there be?

F __ __ __ __ __ s and e __ __ __ __ __ __ __ __ __ s

Matthew 24:8 WHAT are all these things?

The _____ of _____

_____.

WOW! Jesus is sitting on the Mount of Olives when the disciples come to Him and ask Him what the sign will be of His coming and the end of the age. Jesus tells them there will be rumors of wars, wars, famines, earthquakes, and nations rising against nations. He tells them to see that no one misleads or frightens them. WHY aren't the disciples (and us) not to be frightened when we see all these hard and scary things happening around us? All these hard and scary things are signs—the beginning of the end—before Jesus comes again.

The first time Jesus came to earth, it was as our Savior to die on the cross to pay for our sins. After Jesus was resurrected, He left earth to go back to God in heaven. Remember, Jesus told the disciples to take courage and not to let their hearts be troubled, because He was going away to prepare a place for them and He would come back again. Did you know that this hasn't happened yet?

Let's find out about Jesus's Second Coming. In the book of Revelation, God gives the disciple John a vision about Jesus's Second Coming and the things that must take place. Let's find out WHAT God shows John about Jesus's Second Coming. Turn to page 237. Read Revelation 19:11-16. Mark the descriptions of Jesus listed below.

He 　 (His, Himself, Faithful and True, Word of God, King of Kings and LORD of LORDS) (draw a purple cross like this: 　 and color it yellow)

Ask the 5 Ws and an H questions.

Revelation 19:11 WHAT does John see when heaven opens?

_____

Revelation 19:11 WHAT is Jesus called?

_____ and _____

Revelation 19:11 WHAT does Jesus do?

_____

Revelation 19:12 WHAT are Jesus's eyes like?

_____

Revelation 19:12 WHAT is on Jesus's head?

_____

Revelation 19:13 HOW is Jesus clothed?

_____

Revelation 19:13 WHAT is His name called?

_____

Revelation 19:14 WHO is with Jesus?

_____

Revelation 19:15 WHAT comes out of His mouth?

_____

Revelation 19:15 WHAT will Jesus do?

"He may _____ down the

_____, and He will _____ them

with a _____ of _____; and he treads the wine

press of the _____ _____ of
God, the Almighty."

Revelation 19:16 WHAT is the name written on His robe and on His thigh?

_____

Isn't this AWESOME? John sees heaven open and Jesus on a white horse with the armies of heaven (that's us, those of us who have believed in Jesus) clothed in white linen coming with Him. WHAT an AWESOME description of Jesus!

The first time Jesus came to earth, He came as our Savior to pay for our sins. But this time, Jesus is coming as our conquering King! This is our HOPE! When we are afraid, when we are in hard and difficult times, when people are mean, cruel, and rebellious against God, we need to remember these things are only temporary. If we belong to Jesus, He is our HOPE! All power and authority belong to Him. One day soon, Jesus will set up His kingdom on earth and those who believe in Him will rule and reign with Him! WHAT will it be like to live forever with Jesus? We'll find out tomorrow.

Don't forget to say your memory verse! Do not fear! God makes you to dwell in safety!

Jesus is our hope

Can you believe it? This is our last day at Camp Brave-heart. When we got here, we were a little nervous and scared about being far away from home. But God has been with us every day on an awesome adventure as we have learned what the Bible says about being afraid. Since today is our last day, we are going to climb Mount Triumph one more time. But before we do, let's find out WHAT it will be like to live with Jesus in eternity. Pray and thank God for loving and saving you! Ask Him to teach you how to receive His Word, trust Him, and enter into His rest.

Open your Bible and read Revelation 21:1-8, 27.

Ask the 5 Ws and an H questions.

Revelation 21:1 WHAT did John see?

A _____ _____ and a

_____ _____.

Revelation 21:3 WHAT will God do?

He will _____ among men, and they will be His

_____.

Revelation 21:4 WHAT will God do?

He will _____ away every _____ from their

eyes; and there will no longer be *any* _____;

there will no longer be *any* _____, or

_____, or _____.

Revelation 21:5 WHAT does God say?

_____

Revelation 21:5 WHAT are these words?

_____

Revelation 21:7 WHO will inherit these things?

He who _____.

Remember, if you are a believer in Jesus, you are an overcomer! This inheritance is for you!

Revelation 21:7 WHAT will God be to the overcomer?

I will be his _____.

Revelation 21:7 WHAT will the overcomer be to God?

He will be My _____.

Revelation 21:8 WHAT happens to the cowardly and

unbelieving, and abominable, and murderers, and immoral persons, and sorcerers, and idolaters, and all liars?

"Their part *will be* in the _____ that _____

with _____ and _____,

which is the _____ _____."

Revelation 21:27 WHO and WHAT doesn't get to come into the new heaven and earth? "Nothing _____,

and no one who _____

_____ and _____,

shall ever come into it."

Revelation 21:27 WHO gets to come in and live with God and Jesus forever?

"Only those whose _____ are

_____ in the _____

_____ of _____."

Jesus is the Lamb of God! All those who have put their trust in Jesus and who have believed have their names written in the Lamb's Book of Life. Only those believers will be with God and Jesus in the new heaven and earth! There won't be any death, mourning, crying or pain, no murderers, unbelievers, or liars in the new heaven and earth. There won't be any wicked people. The old will pass away, and God will make all things new! Isn't that INCREDIBLE?

In this life there are many scary and difficult things—pain, suffering, sickness, death—because we live in a world broken by sin. BUT we have HOPE! God sent Jesus to rescue us! Jesus loves us so much that He gave His life to save ours. We can take courage, receive comfort, and have cheer because Jesus overcame the world when He died on the cross and rose again. Jesus is our hope! Jesus is coming back for us! The devil wants to defeat us with fear, but we can conquer all our fears when we put our trust in Jesus. Do your hand signal! Faith in Jesus conquers fear! We don't have to be afraid of what is happening to us today, because we know WHO is in control of our future and WHAT awesome plans God has for us!

Read Psalm 4:8—

> In peace I will both lie down and sleep,
> For You alone, O LORD, make me to dwell in safety.

Psalm 4:8 WHAT will God give you so you can lie down and sleep?

_____

Psalm 4:8 HOW will God make you dwell?

In _____

Do you recognize this verse? This is your memory verse. Remember to say it every night before you go to sleep.

Read Hebrews 4:1-3 printed on page 212. Mark these key words.

rest (color it blue)

word (color it green)

faith (believed) (draw a purple book and color it green)

Hebrews 4:1-3

1   Therefore, let us fear if, while a promise remains of entering His rest, any one of you may seem to have come short of it.

2   For indeed we have had good news preached to us, just as they also; but the word they heard did not profit them, because it was not united by faith in those who heard.

3   For we who have believed enter that rest, just as He has said, "As I swore in My wrath, they shall not enter My rest," although His works were finished from the foundation of the world.

Hebrews 4:1 WHAT is there a promise of? Entering

_____ _____.

Hebrews 4:2 WHY didn't this promise profit them?

The w __ __ d they heard was not _____ by
f __ __ __ h.

Hebrews 4:3 WHO has the promise of entering God's rest?

We who have b __ __ __ __ __ __ d.

The way we can enter into God's rest is to take the Word of God and unite (join) it with faith. Take your left hand to represent hearing God's Word, the truth and unite it (put it together) with your right hand to represent faith. Put your hands together like you are praying. Take your united hands and lay them on the side of your face like you are going to sleep to show that:

God's Word + Faith = Rest

Knowing Truth + Believing God = Rest

To enter into God's rest, you have to know the truth—God's Word—and believe it no matter how you feel or what you see.

Read Proverbs 3:5-6.

Proverbs 3:5-6

5   Trust in the LORD with all your heart
     And do not lean on your own
     understanding.

6   In all your ways acknowledge Him
     And He will make your paths straight.

Proverbs 3:5 WHAT are you to do?

_____

Proverbs 3:5 WHAT aren't you to do?

_____

Proverbs 3:6 If you acknowledge God in all your ways, WHAT will God do?

_____

Trust God with all your heart—your entire being. Don't lean on your own understanding. God's ways are much higher than our ways. We may not always understand what God is doing, but we know when we trust God with all our heart, even when we don't understand, He will make our paths straight. God works all things together for our good and to fulfill His purpose.

All right! You did it! You made it to the top of Mount Triumph! Woo-hoo! Let's roast one more marshmallow as you say your memory verse out loud to a grown-up.

Think about all you have learned this week. **WHAT should you do when you are afraid? You need to remember:**

1. **God is in control**—God is with me. God rules over all my circumstances. God had a plan for Joseph, and God has a plan for me. I will trust God.

2. **God causes all things to work together for good**—If I am God's child, God will take the ugly, the bad, the scary, and the things others mean for evil and work it together for my good and His purpose.

3. **Give thanks in everything**—Being thankful puts my focus on God's goodness and not my circumstances. When I am thankful, the God of all peace will give me peace in my heart.

4. **Trust God**—When I trust God, I am like a tree planted by a stream with green leaves bearing fruit even when the hard times come! I will be blessed! God is my God. He will strengthen me, He will help me, and He will uphold me with His righteous right hand. I will trust God with all my heart.

5. **I have hope**—Jesus is coming again! Everyone who puts their trust in Jesus's name is written in the Lamb's Book

of Life. There will be a new heaven and earth! No more death, crying, or pain. God will make all things new!

6. **I can rest**—Knowing truth + Believing God = Rest. God promises that I will lie down and sleep in peace.

All right! Isn't that AWESOME and AMAZING? You have learned how to have a brave heart! You know that there are many scary and difficult things in our broken world: earthquakes, tornados, wars, pandemics, sickness, diseases, and death. Things that upset and worry us. BUT you have learned no matter what happens, you can trust God and Jesus! God will take ALL things—the ugly, the bad, and the scary—and use them for your good and His purpose! You are going to live with Him forever! There will be no more pain, sorrow, or death!

You know WHO God and Jesus are. God is sovereign. God rules and reigns over EVERYTHING! God always does what is right. God has a plan, and no one can stop it. You are to fear God—not man. When you fear man, you are caught in a trap! But the fear of the Lord makes you secure. To fear God is to honor and reverence Him. To listen to and obey Him. Fearing God is the fear that conquers all other fears!

You know Jesus is not only God's Son, but that Jesus is also God. Jesus is God's message to the world. Jesus calmed the sea for the disciples, and He will calm your heart. Jesus has ALL power and authority over everything. Do not let your heart be troubled. When you trust Jesus, He will give you peace that passes all understanding. Jesus is the Prince of Peace.

The very BEST news is that Jesus gave His life to save yours. Jesus is your HOPE! You don't have to be afraid of what is happening to you today, because you know WHO is in control of tomorrow. Just look at HOW God feels about you:

You are chosen.

You are created by God—fearfully (awesomely) and wonderfully made.

You are blessed.

You are adopted as God's child.

You are forgiven.

You have the power of the Holy Spirit.

You have the promise of heaven.

God has good plans for you!

God is for you!

You are LOVED!

One day very soon, heaven will open and Jesus will be back to rule and reign on this earth. All things will be made new. But until Jesus comes, remember:

- **Do not be afraid any longer, only believe.** Faith in Jesus conquers fear. Do your hand signal for faith over fear. Faith in Jesus conquers fear.

- **Remember, God and Jesus love you.** Make a heart with your hands and place it over your heart. God gave His Son to save you!

- **Look up to heaven.** Tell God, *I don't know what to do, but my eyes are on You.* Put your focus on God—not your hard situation.

- **Be strong and courageous.** Do your hand signal. Take your left arm, flex your muscle, and say "Be strong." Now lift your right arm, flex that muscle, and say "and courageous," to remind you to hold on to God. You are not alone. God will not leave you!

- **Rest.** Take your left hand and put it together with your right hand like you are praying. Take your united hands and lay them on the side of your face like you are going to sleep. Lay your head down on your hands and rest in God. God's Word + Faith = Rest.

Way to go! No matter what happens, keep your eyes on God! God and Jesus love you! WHAT is the ONLY way to have a brave heart? When I am afraid, I will put my trust in God!

PUZZLE ANSWERS

Page 16

Jesus

Page 19

"Do not be afraid any longer, only believe." Mark 5:36

Page 48

"When I am afraid, I will put my trust in You." Psalm 56:3

Page 57

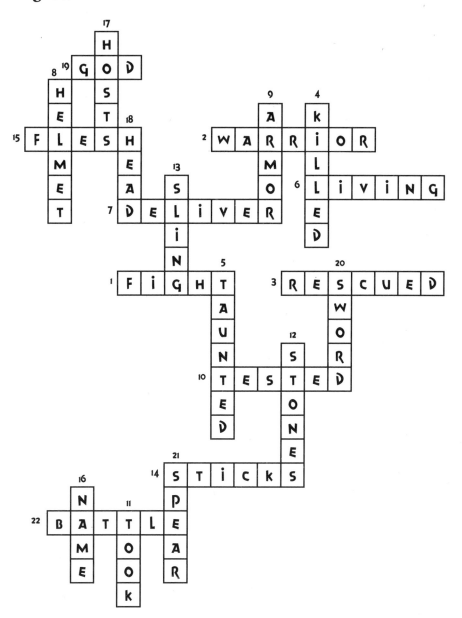

Page 79

"In this is love, not that we loved God, but that He loved us and sent His Son *to be* the propitiation for our sins." 1 John 4:10

Page 90

C	A	D	O	P	T	I	O	N	J	D	E	V	A	S
L	H	G	I	F	T	E	H	E	A	V	E	N	L	Y
T	O	O	A	S	M	L	S	A	J	Q	D	T	I	O
Z	V	V	S	B	V	U	K	I	N	D	Q	S	G	B
I	K	J	E	E	S	K	R	O	W	H	D	I	N	Z
F	A	H	L	E	R	O	F	E	B	T	W	R	I	S
O	N	O	I	T	N	E	T	N	I	I	H	S	S	S
U	H	G	U	O	R	H	T	F	R	A	L	C	S	S
N	L	A	U	T	I	R	I	P	S	F	L	L	E	E
D	G	O	D	V	G	V	J	L	V	O	O	K	L	L
A	O	P	I	H	S	N	A	M	K	R	O	W	B	E
T	O	Q	Q	T	G	R	A	C	E	S	B	W	V	M
I	D	N	P	L	A	C	E	S	H	J	O	E	Q	A
O	H	O	L	Y	M	S	K	M	L	X	R	N	J	L
N	M	O	W	O	R	L	D	G	N	Y	C	Q	S	B

Page 115

"You who fear the LORD, trust in the LORD; He is their help and their shield." Psalm 115:11

Page 148

"Have I not commanded you? Be strong and courageous! Do not tremble or be dismayed, for the LORD your God is with you wherever you go." Joshua 1:9

Page 156

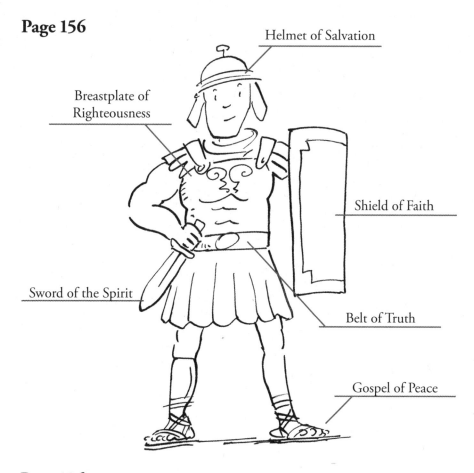

Helmet of Salvation

Breastplate of
Righteousness

Shield of Faith

Sword of the Spirit

Belt of Truth

Gospel of Peace

Page 186

"In peace I will both lie down and sleep, For You alone, O
LORD, make me to dwell in safety." Psalm 4:8

Page 198

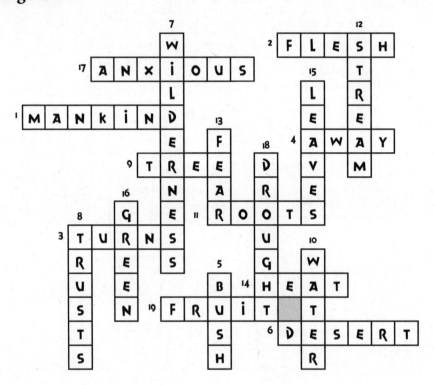

OBSERVATION WORKSHEETS

JOHN 1:1-2, 14

1 In the beginning was the Word, and the Word was with God, and the Word was God.

2 He was in the beginning with God.

14 And the Word became flesh, and dwelt among us; and we saw His glory, glory as of the only begotten from the Father, full of grace and truth.

JOHN 1:28-29

28 These things took place in Bethany beyond the Jordan, where John was baptizing.

29 The next day he saw Jesus coming to him and said, "Behold, the Lamb of God who takes away the sin of the world!"

MARK 4:1-2

1 He began to teach again by the sea. And such a very large crowd gathered to Him that He got into a boat in the sea and sat down; and the whole crowd was by the sea on the land.

2 And He was teaching them many things in parables, and was saying to them in His teaching,

MARK 4:35-41

35 On that day, when evening came, He said to them, "Let us go over to the other side."

36 Leaving the crowd, they took Him along with them in the boat, just as He was; and other boats were with Him.

37 And there arose a fierce gale of wind, and the waves were breaking over the boat so much that the boat was already filling up.

38 Jesus Himself was in the stern, asleep on the cushion; and they woke Him and said to Him, "Teacher, do You not care that we are perishing?"

39 And He got up and rebuked the wind and said to the sea, "Hush, be still." And the wind died down and it became perfectly calm.

40 And He said to them, "Why are you afraid? Do you still have no faith?"

41 They became very much afraid and said to one another, "Who then is this, that even the wind and the sea obey Him?"

MATTHEW 14:22-33

22 Immediately He made the disciples get into the boat and go ahead of Him to the other side, while He sent the crowds away.

23 After He had sent the crowds away, He went up on the mountain by Himself to pray; and when it was evening, He was there alone.

24 But the boat was already a long distance from the land, battered by the waves; for the wind was contrary.

25 And in the fourth watch of the night He came to them, walking on the sea.

26 When the disciples saw Him walking on the sea, they were terrified, and said, "It is a ghost!" And they cried out in fear.

27 But immediately Jesus spoke to them, saying, "Take courage, it is I; do not be afraid."

28 Peter said to Him, "Lord, if it is You, command me to come to You on the water."

29 And He said, "Come!" And Peter got out of the boat, and walked on the water and came toward Jesus.

30 But seeing the wind, he became frightened, and beginning to sink, he cried out, "Lord, save me!"

31 Immediately Jesus stretched out His hand and took hold of him, and said to him, "You of little faith, why did you doubt?"

32 When they got into the boat, the wind stopped.

33 And those who were in the boat worshiped Him, saying, "You are certainly God's Son!"

1 SAMUEL 17

1 Now the Philistines gathered their armies for battle; and they were gathered at Socoh which belongs to Judah, and they camped between Socoh and Azekah, in Ephes-dammim.

2 Saul and the men of Israel were gathered and camped in the valley of Elah, and drew up in battle array to encounter the Philistines.

3 The Philistines stood on the mountain on one side while Israel stood on the mountain on the other side, with the valley between them.

4 Then a champion came out from the armies of the Philistines named Goliath, from Gath, whose height was six cubits and a span.

5 *He had* a bronze helmet on his head, and he was clothed with scale-armor which weighed five thousand shekels of bronze.

6 *He* also *had* bronze greaves on his legs and a bronze javelin *slung* between his shoulders.

7 The shaft of his spear was like a weaver's beam, and the head of his spear *weighed* six hundred shekels of iron; his shield-carrier also walked before him.

8 He stood and shouted to the ranks of Israel and said to them, "Why do you come out to draw up in battle array? Am I not the Philistine and you servants of Saul? Choose a man for yourselves and let him come down to me.

9 If he is able to fight with me and kill me, then we will become your servants; but if I prevail against him and kill him, then you shall become our servants and serve us."

10   Again the Philistine said, "I defy the ranks of Israel this day; give me a man that we may fight together."

11   When Saul and all Israel heard these words of the Philistine, they were dismayed and greatly afraid.

12   Now David was the son of the Ephrathite of Bethlehem in Judah, whose name was Jesse, and he had eight sons. And Jesse was old in the days of Saul, advanced *in years* among men.

13   The three older sons of Jesse had gone after Saul to the battle. And the names of his three sons who went to the battle were Eliab the firstborn, and the second to him Abinadab, and the third Shammah.

14   David was the youngest. Now the three oldest followed Saul,

15   but David went back and forth from Saul to tend his father's flock at Bethlehem.

16   The Philistine came forward morning and evening for forty days and took his stand.

17   Then Jesse said to David his son, "Take now for your brothers an ephah of this roasted grain and these ten loaves and run to the camp to your brothers.

18   Bring also these ten cuts of cheese to the commander of *their* thousand, and look into the welfare of your brothers, and bring back news of them.

19   For Saul and they and all the men of Israel are in the valley of Elah, fighting with the Philistines."

20   So David arose early in the morning and left the flock with a keeper and took *the supplies* and went as Jesse had commanded him. And he came to the circle of the camp while the army was going out in battle array shouting the war cry.

21   Israel and the Philistines drew up in battle array, army against army.

22   Then David left his baggage in the care of the baggage keeper, and ran to the battle line and entered in order to greet his brothers.

23   As he was talking with them, behold, the champion, the Philistine from Gath named Goliath, was coming up from the army of the Philistines, and he spoke these same words; and David heard *them*.

24   When all the men of Israel saw the man, they fled from him and were greatly afraid.

25   The men of Israel said, "Have you seen this man who is coming up? Surely he is coming up to defy Israel. And it will be that the king will enrich the man who kills him with great riches and will give him his daughter and make his father's house free in Israel."

26   Then David spoke to the men who were standing by him, saying, "What will be done for the man who kills this Philistine and takes away the reproach from Israel? For who is this uncircumcised Philistine, that he should taunt the armies of the living God?"

27   The people answered him in accord with this word, saying, "Thus it will be done for the man who kills him."

28   Now Eliab his oldest brother heard when he spoke to the men; and Eliab's anger burned against David and he said, "Why have you come down? And with whom have you left those few sheep in the wilderness? I know your insolence and the wickedness of your heart; for you have come down in order to see the battle."

29   But David said, "What have I done now? Was it not just a question?"

30   Then he turned away from him to another and said the same thing; and the people answered the same thing as before.

31   When the words which David spoke were heard, they told *them* to Saul, and he sent for him.

32   David said to Saul, "Let no man's heart fail on account of him; your servant will go and fight with this Philistine."

33   Then Saul said to David, "You are not able to go against this Philistine to fight with him; for you are *but* a youth while he has been a warrior from his youth."

34   But David said to Saul, "Your servant was tending his father's sheep. When a lion or a bear came and took a lamb from the flock,

35   I went out after him and attacked him, and rescued *it* from his mouth; and when he rose up against me, I seized *him* by his beard and struck him and killed him.

36   Your servant has killed both the lion and the bear; and this

uncircumcised Philistine will be like one of them, since he has taunted the armies of the living God."

37 And David said, "The LORD who delivered me from the paw of the lion and from the paw of the bear, He will deliver me from the hand of this Philistine." And Saul said to David, "Go, and may the LORD be with you."

38 Then Saul clothed David with his garments and put a bronze helmet on his head, and he clothed him with armor.

39 David girded his sword over his armor and tried to walk, for he had not tested *them*. So David said to Saul, "I cannot go with these, for I have not tested *them*." And David took them off.

40 He took his stick in his hand and chose for himself five smooth stones from the brook, and put them in the shepherd's bag which he had, even in *his* pouch, and his sling was in his hand; and he approached the Philistine.

41 Then the Philistine came on and approached David, with the shield-bearer in front of him.

42 When the Philistine looked and saw David, he disdained him; for he was *but* a youth, and ruddy, with a handsome appearance.

43 The Philistine said to David, "Am I a dog, that you come to me with sticks?" And the Philistine cursed David by his gods.

44 The Philistine also said to David, "Come to me, and I will give your flesh to the birds of the sky and the beasts of the field."

45 Then David said to the Philistine, "You come to me with a sword, a spear, and a javelin, but I come to you in the name of the LORD of hosts, the God of the armies of Israel, whom you have taunted.

46 This day the LORD will deliver you up into my hands, and I will strike you down and remove your head from you. And I will give the dead bodies of the army of the Philistines this day to the birds of the sky and the wild beasts of the earth, that all the earth may know that there is a God in Israel,

47 and that all this assembly may know that the LORD does not deliver

by sword or by spear; for the battle is the LORD's and He will give you into our hands."

48 Then it happened when the Philistine rose and came and drew near to meet David, that David ran quickly toward the battle line to meet the Philistine.

49 And David put his hand into his bag and took from it a stone and slung *it*, and struck the Philistine on his forehead. And the stone sank into his forehead, so that he fell on his face to the ground.

50 Thus David prevailed over the Philistine with a sling and a stone, and he struck the Philistine and killed him; but there was no sword in David's hand.

51 Then David ran and stood over the Philistine and took his sword and drew it out of its sheath and killed him, and cut off his head with it. When the Philistines saw that their champion was dead, they fled.

52 The men of Israel and Judah arose and shouted and pursued the Philistines as far as the valley, and to the gates of Ekron. And the slain Philistines lay along the way to Shaaraim, even to Gath and Ekron.

53 The sons of Israel returned from chasing the Philistines and plundered their camps.

54 Then David took the Philistine's head and brought it to Jerusalem, but he put his weapons in his tent.

55 Now when Saul saw David going out against the Philistine, he said to Abner the commander of the army, "Abner, whose son is this young man?" And Abner said, "By your life, O king, I do not know."

56 The king said, "You inquire whose son the youth is."

57 So when David returned from killing the Philistine, Abner took him and brought him before Saul with the Philistine's head in his hand.

58 Saul said to him, "Whose son are you, young man?" And David answered, "*I am* the son of your servant Jesse the Bethlehemite."

psalm 139:1-18

1 O Lord, You have searched me and known *me*.

2 You know when I sit down and when I rise up;
   You understand my thought from afar.

3 You scrutinize my path and my lying down,
   And are intimately acquainted with all my ways.

4 Even before there is a word on my tongue,
   Behold, O Lord, You know it all.

5 You have enclosed me behind and before,
   And laid Your hand upon me.

6 *Such* knowledge is too wonderful for me;
   It is *too* high, I cannot attain to it.

7 Where can I go from Your Spirit?
   Or where can I flee from Your presence?

8 If I ascend to heaven, You are there;
   If I make my bed in Sheol, behold, You are there.

9 If I take the wings of the dawn,
   If I dwell in the remotest part of the sea,

10 Even there Your hand will lead me,
    And Your right hand will lay hold of me.

11 If I say, "Surely the darkness will overwhelm me,
    And the light around me will be night,"

12 Even the darkness is not dark to You,
    And the night is as bright as the day.
    Darkness and light are alike *to You*.

13 For You formed my inward parts;
    You wove me in my mother's womb.

14 I will give thanks to You, for I am fearfully and wonderfully made;
    Wonderful are Your works,
    And my soul knows it very well.

15 My frame was not hidden from You,
    When I was made in secret,
    And skillfully wrought in the depths of the earth;

16 Your eyes have seen my unformed substance;
And in Your book were all written
The days that were ordained *for me*,
When as yet there was not one of them.

17 How precious also are Your thoughts to me, O God!
How vast is the sum of them!

18 If I should count them, they would outnumber the sand.
When I awake, I am still with You.

JOHN 3:16-17

16 For God so loved the world, that He gave His only begotten Son, that whoever believes in Him shall not perish, but have eternal life.

17 For God did not send the Son into the world to judge the world, but that the world might be saved through Him.

2 CHRONICLES 20:1-30

1 Now it came about after this that the sons of Moab and the sons of Ammon, together with some of the Meunites, came to make war against Jehoshaphat.

2 Then some came and reported to Jehoshaphat, saying, "A great multitude is coming against you from beyond the sea, out of Aram and behold, they are in Hazazon-tamar (that is Engedi)."

3 Jehoshaphat was afraid and turned his attention to seek the LORD, and proclaimed a fast throughout all Judah.

4 So Judah gathered together to seek help from the LORD; they even came from all the cities of Judah to seek the LORD.

5 Then Jehoshaphat stood in the assembly of Judah and Jerusalem, in the house of the LORD before the new court,

6 and he said, "O LORD, the God of our fathers, are You not God in the heavens? And are You not ruler over all the kingdoms of the nations? Power and might are in Your hand so that no one can stand against You.

7 Did You not, O our God, drive out the inhabitants of this land

before Your people Israel and give it to the descendants of Abraham Your friend forever?

8 They have lived in it, and have built You a sanctuary there for Your name, saying,

9 'Should evil come upon us, the sword, *or* judgment, or pestilence, or famine, we will stand before this house and before You (for Your name is in this house) and cry to You in our distress, and You will hear and deliver *us.*'

10 Now behold, the sons of Ammon and Moab and Mount Seir, whom You did not let Israel invade when they came out of the land of Egypt (they turned aside from them and did not destroy them),

11 see *how* they are rewarding us by coming to drive us out from Your possession which You have given us as an inheritance.

12 O our God, will You not judge them? For we are powerless before this great multitude who are coming against us; nor do we know what to do, but our eyes are on You."

13 All Judah was standing before the LORD, with their infants, their wives and their children.

14 Then in the midst of the assembly the Spirit of the LORD came upon Jahaziel the son of Zechariah, the son of Benaiah, the son of Jeiel, the son of Mattaniah, the Levite of the sons of Asaph;

15 and he said, "Listen, all Judah and the inhabitants of Jerusalem and King Jehoshaphat: thus says the LORD to you, 'Do not fear or be dismayed because of this great multitude, for the battle is not yours but God's.

16 Tomorrow go down against them. Behold, they will come up by the ascent of Ziz, and you will find them at the end of the valley in front of the wilderness of Jeruel.

17 You *need* not fight in this *battle*; station yourselves, stand and see the salvation of the LORD on your behalf, O Judah and Jerusalem.' Do not fear or be dismayed; tomorrow go out to face them, for the LORD is with you."

18 Jehoshaphat bowed his head with *his* face to the ground, and all

Judah and the inhabitants of Jerusalem fell down before the LORD, worshiping the LORD.

19   The Levites, from the sons of the Kohathites and of the sons of the Korahites, stood up to praise the LORD God of Israel, with a very loud voice.

20   They rose early in the morning and went out to the wilderness of Tekoa; and when they went out, Jehoshaphat stood and said, "Listen to me, O Judah and inhabitants of Jerusalem, put your trust in the LORD your God and you will be established. Put your trust in His prophets and succeed."

21   When he had consulted with the people, he appointed those who sang to the LORD and those who praised *Him* in holy attire, as they went out before the army and said, "Give thanks to the LORD, for His lovingkindness is everlasting."

22   When they began singing and praising, the LORD set ambushes against the sons of Ammon, Moab and Mount Seir, who had come against Judah; so they were routed.

23   For the sons of Ammon and Moab rose up against the inhabitants of Mount Seir destroying *them* completely; and when they had finished with the inhabitants of Seir, they helped to destroy one another.

24   When Judah came to the lookout of the wilderness, they looked toward the multitude, and behold, they *were* corpses lying on the ground, and no one had escaped.

25   When Jehoshaphat and his people came to take their spoil, they found much among them, *including* goods, garments and valuable things which they took for themselves, more than they could carry. And they were three days taking the spoil because there was so much.

26   Then on the fourth day they assembled in the valley of Beracah, for there they blessed the LORD. Therefore they have named that place "The Valley of Beracah" until today.

27   Every man of Judah and Jerusalem returned with Jehoshaphat at their head, returning to Jerusalem with joy, for the LORD had made them to rejoice over their enemies.

28 They came to Jerusalem with harps, lyres and trumpets to the house of the LORD.

29 And the dread of God was on all the kingdoms of the lands when they heard that the LORD had fought against the enemies of Israel.

30 So the kingdom of Jehoshaphat was at peace, for his God gave him rest on all sides.

JOSHUA 1:1-9

1 Now it came about after the death of Moses the servant of the LORD, that the LORD spoke to Joshua the son of Nun, Moses' servant, saying,

2 "Moses My servant is dead; now therefore arise, cross this Jordan, you and all this people, to the land which I am giving to them, to the sons of Israel.

3 Every place on which the sole of your foot treads, I have given it to you, just as I spoke to Moses.

4 From the wilderness and this Lebanon, even as far as the great river, the river Euphrates, all the land of the Hittites, and as far as the Great Sea toward the setting of the sun will be your territory.

5 No man will *be able to* stand before you all the days of your life. Just as I have been with Moses, I will be with you; I will not fail you or forsake you.

6 Be strong and courageous, for you shall give this people possession of the land which I swore to their fathers to give them.

7 Only be strong and very courageous; be careful to do according to all the law which Moses My servant commanded you; do not turn from it to the right or to the left, so that you may have success wherever you go.

8 This book of the law shall not depart from your mouth, but you shall meditate on it day and night, so that you may be careful to do according to all that is written in it; for then you will make your way prosperous, and then you will have success.

9   Have I not commanded you? Be strong and courageous! Do not tremble or be dismayed, for the LORD your God is with you wherever you go."

EPHESIANS 6:10-18

10   Finally, be strong in the Lord and in the strength of His might.

11   Put on the full armor of God, so that you will be able to stand firm against the schemes of the devil.

12   For our struggle is not against flesh and blood, but against the rulers, against the powers, against the world forces of this darkness, against the spiritual *forces* of wickedness in the heavenly *places.*

13   Therefore, take up the full armor of God, so that you will be able to resist in the evil day, and having done everything, to stand firm.

14   Stand firm therefore, HAVING GIRDED YOUR LOINS WITH TRUTH, and HAVING PUT ON THE BREASTPLATE OF RIGHTEOUSNESS,

15   and having shod YOUR FEET WITH THE PREPARATION OF THE GOSPEL OF PEACE;

16   in addition to all, taking up the shield of faith with which you will be able to extinguish all the flaming arrows of the evil *one.*

17   And take THE HELMET OF SALVATION, and the sword of the Spirit, which is the word of God.

18   With all prayer and petition pray at all times in the Spirit, and with this in view, be on the alert with all perseverance and petition for all the saints,

JOHN 14:1-3, 27

1   Do not let your heart be troubled; believe in God, believe also in Me.

2   In My Father's house are many rooms; if *that* were not *so,* I would have told you, because I am going *there* to prepare a place for you.

3   And if I go and prepare a place for you, I am coming again and will take you to Myself, so that where I am, *there* you also will be.

27   Peace I leave you, My peace I give you; not as the world gives, do I give to you. Do not let your hearts be troubled, nor fearful.

PHILIPPIANS 4:6-13

6   Be anxious for nothing, but in everything by prayer and supplication with thanksgiving let your requests be made known to God.

7   And the peace of God, which surpasses all comprehension, will guard your hearts and your minds in Christ Jesus.

8   Finally, brethren, whatever is true, whatever is honorable, whatever is right, whatever is pure, whatever is lovely, whatever is of good repute, if there is any excellence and if anything worthy of praise, dwell on these things.

9   The things you have learned and received and heard and seen in me, practice these things, and the God of peace will be with you.

10   But I rejoiced in the Lord greatly, that now at last you have revived your concern for me; indeed, you were concerned *before*, but you lacked opportunity.

11   Not that I speak from want, for I have learned to be content in whatever circumstances I am.

12   I know how to get along with humble means, and I also know how to live in prosperity; in any and every circumstance I have learned the secret of being filled and going hungry, both of having abundance and suffering need.

13   I can do all things through Him who strengthens me.

GENESIS 39:1-6

1   Now Joseph had been taken down to Egypt; and Potiphar, an Egyptian officer of Pharaoh, the captain of the bodyguard, bought him from the Ishmaelites, who had taken him down there.

2   The Lord was with Joseph, so he became a successful man. And he was in the house of his master, the Egyptian.

3   Now his master saw that the LORD was with him and *how* the LORD caused all that he did to prosper in his hand.

4   So Joseph found favor in his sight and became his personal servant; and he made him overseer over his house, and all that he owned he put in his charge.

5   It came about that from the time he made him overseer in his house and over all that he owned, the LORD blessed the Egyptian's house on account of Joseph; thus the LORD's blessing was upon all that he owned, in the house and in the field.

6   So he left everything he owned in Joseph's charge; and with him *there* he did not concern himself with anything except the food which he ate. Now Joseph was handsome in form and appearance.

MATTHEW 24:3-8

3   As He was sitting on the Mount of Olives, the disciples came to Him privately, saying, "Tell us, when will these things happen, and what *will be* the sign of Your coming, and of the end of the age?"

4   And Jesus answered and said to them, "See to it that no one misleads you.

5   For many will come in My name, saying, 'I am the Christ,' and will mislead many.

6   You will be hearing of wars and rumors of wars. See that you are not frightened, for *those things* must take place, but *that* is not yet the end.

7   For nation will rise against nation, and kingdom against kingdom, and in various places there will be famines and earthquakes.

8   But all these things are *merely* the beginning of birth pangs."

REVELATION 19:11-16

11   And I saw heaven opened, and behold, a white horse, and He who sat on it *is* called Faithful and True, and in righteousness He judges and wages war.

12 His eyes *are* a flame of fire, and on His head *are* many diadems; and He has a name written *on Him* which no one knows except Himself.

13 *He is* clothed with a robe dipped in blood, and His name is called The Word of God.

14 And the armies which are in heaven, clothed in fine linen, white *and* clean, were following Him on white horses.

15 From His mouth comes a sharp sword, so that with it He may strike down the nations, and He will rule them with a rod of iron; and He treads the wine press of the fierce wrath of God, the Almighty.

16 And on His robe and on His thigh He has a name written, "KING OF KINGS, AND LORD OF LORDS."

DiSCOVER 4 YOURSELF!®

Kay Arthur and Cyndy Shearer

ISBN 978-0-7369-0119-2

Kay Arthur, Janna Arndt,
Lisa Guest, and Cyndy Shearer

ISBN 978-0-7369-0144-4

Kay Arthur and Janna Arndt

ISBN 978-0-7369-0148-2

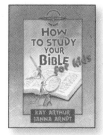

Kay Arthur and Janna Arndt

ISBN 978-0-7369-0362-2

Kay Arthur and Janna Arndt

ISBN 978-0-7369-0546-6

Kay Arthur and Scoti Domeij

ISBN 978-0-7369-0203-8

Kay Arthur and Janna Arndt

ISBN 978-0-7369-0374-5

Kay Arthur and Janna Arndt

ISBN 978-0-7369-0143-7

Kay Arthur and Janna Arndt

ISBN 978-0-7369-0666-1

Kay Arthur and Janna Arndt

ISBN 978-0-7369-0936-5

Kay Arthur and Janna Arndt

ISBN 978-0-7369-0739-2

Kay Arthur and Janna Arndt

ISBN 978-0-7369-1161-0

Kay Arthur and Janna Arndt

ISBN 978-0-7369-0937-2

Kay Arthur and Janna Arndt

ISBN 978-0-7369-1527-4

Kay Arthur and Janna Arndt

ISBN 978-0-7369-2036-0

Kay Arthur and Janna Arndt

ISBN 978-0-7369-0147-5